A PENSIONER VISITS PERU

PETER S FARLEY

COPYRIGHT

ACKNOWLEDGEMENTS

The author wishes to thank Viator.com tour organisers for their professional service during his Peruvian tour. A special thank you is extended to Brian Mills who worked on the cover design for this book. [www.bmillsdesigns.co.uk]

DEDICATION

This book is dedicated to the people and the Government of Peru. They helped to make the author's visit to their country both pleasant and memorable.

ABOUT THE AUTHOR

Born and raised in England the author has also lived for some years in the Republic of South Africa. He holds a BA (Hons) Degree awarded by Liverpool University and has written articles for various publications. These include *The Titanic Chronicle*, (RSA) *The Roodepoort Record*, (RSA) *The Messenger*, (UK) and *The Turton Tower Newsletter*, (UK). The author has published two books titled *Mysterious Tales from Turton Tower* and *The Red Tabs*.

TABLE OF CONTENTS

INTRODUCTION
★★★★★★★★★★★★

Throughout the years my upload of self made travel videos, to the internet site of YouTube, have provoked some measure of interest. One of them in particular has the title of 'Two brothers visit Isandhlwana and Rorke's Drift.' It tells the tale about two men, who happen to be brothers and who visit the famous historical sites. The reader may remember it was at Rorke's Drift, in the year 1879, when about 130 of Queen Victoria's soldiers fought off an attack by an estimated four thousand Zulu warriors. As a result of this conflict, some eleven Victoria Crosses were awarded to the Queen's combatants. They were the highest number to be awarded in any one campaign. Anyway, this is to say that my uploaded video has been viewed more than eight thousand times! In passing, I like to think they were not all made by the same person!

In addition to the viewings, many people posted comments about my creations and I'm pleased to say that most of them had a positive bias. However, there was one that commented on the mediocre quality of the Rorke's Drift production. I had to admit that it wasn't up to the standard of my later offerings. But as I explained to the complainant, my video equipment wasn't of the best at the time of the recording. The reply was that it didn't matter too much because as it was, I was providing something that was at least watchable. But more importantly, I was giving the people who were not able to visit such places, an opportunity to see them. Albeit if only on a computer monitor. It occurred to me that besides making videos, I could also write about my travels.

Consequently whoever reads my work might be motivated into making a similar journey. At the very least my reports might hopefully provide some entertaining reading. From this thought emerged the idea of 'A Pensioner Visits Peru.'

On the run-up to retiring from my working life friends would say, "You will soon be able to do all the things that you ever wanted to do and visit all the places you ever wanted to see. What's more you will have all the time in the world to do it."

I finally retired from a working life of over fifty years. Getting out of bed each morning and making my way to work and in all kinds of weather, had become a habit. It was of course a habit that was essential to sustain my life and also to finance some limited pleasure. Now it was all finished and what I had to show for my years of labour was time to spare and some money saved up. However, I'm not sure if the quantities of time and money were equally balanced. In any event, it was an opportunity to consider how I was going to spend the few remaining years of my life.

I had often fantasized over the idea of travelling to South America. There was something about the continent that appealed to my Latin nature. They speak Spanish there don't they? But more than that, they have some historical sites that are worthy of a visit. In particular there is a place in Peru called Machu Picchu. Essentially it is a mountain fastness where the legendary Incas lived. All very exciting. But coupled with that there is the warm climate, the good food, the open spaces and many interesting people.

There was a famous Chinese philosopher named Lao – Tzu, who at some point in his lifetime coined the phrase,

"A journey of a thousand miles begins with a single step."[1] *When he spoke those immortal words I wonder if he had just retired from his full time work and was contemplating a lengthy vacation? Either way, what he said is true. Every journey does indeed begin with a first step. But I would like to add a little more to his philosophy. Every journey also begins with an IDEA!*

Yes, usually the idea comes first and then the steps of the journey follow on. So with South America in mind, at least I had an idea. But what came next was to take that first step.

My idea was to travel to Peru, the mysterious country located in the western part of South America. It wasn't a random idea. I had pondered and day-dreamed about Peru for many months. Now the opportunity was ripe. That simple fact was plain enough. But a question needed to be answered. How was I going to take my first step?

I was living in a North of England town and my status was that of a single person and a pensioner to boot. Additionally I had no travelling companion(s) with which to share my thoughts and experiences. How on earth was I going to overcome the fears and doubts of travelling alone? It might have been one small step for an ancient Chinaman but this was a giant leap for a pensioner!

In the following pages I shall explain how I took that first step and how I made my day-dream become a reality.

THE FIRST STEP

Before continuing let me share a little story. It is about a community of earwigs that lived in woodland, at the base of a hill. Yes, the wording is correct; I did say "earwigs." In the woodland was a certain tree that towered above the height of the others. One day the earwigs decided to organise a race. A lovely prize was offered for the first earwig to climb to the top of the tallest tree. On the day when the race began, a large crowd of insects gathered around the tall tree. The contestants were given the instruction to begin and thereafter started to climb. At first it was easy, since they were fresh and full of energy. Also the crowd offered their support by cheering them on.

In all honesty not one insect really believed that the earwigs would reach the top of the tall tree. Specific utterances could be heard above the general murmur of the crowd. Comments like, "They will never make it to the top!" and "Oh, that's way too difficult a climb." One insect even shouted, "There's not a chance that they will succeed. The tree is far too high!"

After a few minutes some of the earwigs began to falter and fall off the tree. The remainder, having seen the fate of their fellow competitors, tightened their grip and with grim determination tried harder. The crowd of insects were now some distance below the earwigs. They were heard to shout, "It's far too difficult no one will make it to the top, better to give up now!" Hearing these words more earwigs began to falter and fall from the tree. The crowd shouted tauntingly, "Here wig-go" and laughed at their downfall. However, one particular earwig pressed on relentlessly. He climbed higher and higher. At the end of the day he was the only one to make it to the top of the tree. The crowd and the other contestants gazed in astonishment.

Much later at the prize giving ceremony, everyone gathered around the winner. They wanted to know how he had managed to complete the climb. With a broad smile across his face, the tiny earwig openly announced that he was in fact practically **DEAF!!**

The wisdom of this fictitious story is to **never listen to other people's negative comments. If you do, you run the risk of having your most wonderful dreams taken away from you. The ones you have nurtured in your heart.**
Always remember that words have power. Everything that you hear and everything that you read will affect your actions. Therefore always strive to be **POSITIVE** *and above all, be practically* **DEAF** *when people tell you that you cannot fulfil* **YOUR** *dreams. Tell yourself constantly:* **I CAN DO THIS!!!**

Evil Knievel was a world famous American stunt rider and in October of 1975 he performed one of his most famous stunts. He rode his motorcycle up a ramp and 'flew' through the air clearing fourteen parked Greyhound buses. Towards the end of his career this is what he had to say to his admirers: **"Follow your dreams; that is what life is all about."** [2]

In a nutshell, the advice to be gleaned from this little story is as follows.
BE PRACTICALLY DEAF *to other people's negative comments and* **FOLLOW YOUR DREAMS.**

Now that I have shared that golden advice let me explain how I made my dream come true and how I lived it. But please remember, **YOU** *can also make* **YOUR** *dream come true!!*

****

PLANNING THE DREAM

****

Travelling with an organised tour group is normally not my cup of tea. I usually find that the time allowed to visit places of interest is limited. The group members listen to a guide who recites set pieces of information. After which and before looking at any place in detail, the group is requested to move on. They are harried along like a herd of cattle and then instructed to stop at the next objective. To me the whole episode is reminiscent of a military operation. With this idea in mind I was somewhat reluctant to book with a tour company.

However, on this occasion there was one major reason for doing so. I would be travelling alone. But more importantly, to a land where English is sparsely spoken and just as sparsely understood. I eventually decided it would be a good idea to join a tour. After all, I reasoned that the people on the tour would mostly speak English and that the tour agency would cater for such a group. Coupled with that I assumed the people would have a like interest in the places being visited and perhaps dictate the pace.

After much deliberation, I planned to book with an organised tour for the first of a two week vacation and to leave the second week open. It was my intention to fill the second week with visits to places of my choice or just to chill out. Once my brain had ratified this idea I proceeded to surf the internet in search of a suitable provider. Using the Google search engine my fingers typed the words 'Cheap tours in Peru.' Hey presto! To my great joy a variety of offers came into view. After studying the various dates and prices, I finally chose the following printed itinerary. It hails from the web page of www. Viator Tours.com, the worldwide tour operators.

8-Day Best of Peru Tour: Lima, Cusco, Paracas, Nazca Lines and Machu Picchu

Location: Lima, Peru.
Duration: 8 days (approx)
Tour Code: 5243NAZMP
From GBP £907.91

Activity Info:

Make the most of your South America vacation with this 8-day best of Peru tour!
While Peru boasts many archaeological sites and fascinating cities, this tour covers the essentials: Lima, Cusco, Paracas, and the Nazca Lines and, of course, Machu Picchu.
With both guided tours and leisure time throughout your trip, this 8-day itinerary fits the budget while satisfying your need to explore!

Highlights:

8-day tour of Lima, Cusco, Nazca Lines and Machu Picchu
Spend a day in Lima exploring its natural parks and archaeological sites
Hop on an air tour for a bird's-eye view of the Nazca Lines
Explore Machu Picchu, one of the New Seven Wonders of the World and a UNESCO World Heritage Site
All accommodation, breakfast and tours included.
Book this 8-day tour of Lima, Nazca, Paracas and Cusco, and leave the stress of daily schedules, road transportation and hotel options behind!
This great-value tour covers all the details and allows you to make the most of your vacation in Peru.
Designed for both first-time visitors and savvy travellers alike, the tour includes your hotel accommodation (with breakfast), transfers to and from the airports in Lima and Cusco, guided tours and much more!
You'll first spend some time exploring Lima – the City of Kings and capital of Peru. Enjoy a guided sightseeing tour of both the ancient and modern sides of the city, its nature parks and archaeological wonders.

You'll also have the opportunity to visit the San Francisco convent, home to Lima's mysterious catacombs.

Then it's on to the city of Nazca for an air tour over the mysterious Nazca Lines. You'll enjoy the views aboard a small Cessna aeroplane, which has a window seat for every passenger. The spectacular views of the famous geoglyphs are available only from the air!

On your way back to Lima from Nazca, you'll make an overnight stop in Paracas and spend the morning cruising around the Ballestas Islands on a boat tour. Get up close and personal with wildlife and gain panoramic coastal views of Peru's shoreline and the mysterious Chandelier.

After an overnight stay in Lima, you'll board your flight to Cusco (flight not included in tour price). You'll have two full days to explore Cusco (with both guided tours and leisure time) and one full day at Machu Picchu, one of the New Seven Wonders of the World and a UNESCO World Heritage Site.

IMPORTANT: Please provide passport details for all travellers at the time of booking. Failure to do so may result in your tour not being confirmed.

Departure Point: Tour departs from the International Airport in Lima and coincides with your flight's arrival

Departure Time: Coincides with your flight's arrival in Lima

Duration: 8days (approx.)

Tour and Pricing Options: Our pricing is constantly updated to ensure you always receive the lowest price possible - we 100% guarantee it.

Tour options: Economy Class Single Room Code: ECOSIN Economy class single room.

The number of adults selected corresponds to the number of single rooms requested (e.g. select 1 adult to book 1 room, 2 adults to book 2 rooms, etc).

Price from GBP £907.91

Economy Class Double Room Code: ECODBL Economy class double room.

The number of adults selected corresponds to the number of double

rooms requested (e.g. select 1 adult to book 1 room, 2 adults to book 2 rooms, etc).
Price from GBP *£1,450.14*
First Class Single Room Code: FIRSIN First class single room. The number of adults selected corresponds to the number of single rooms requested (e.g. select 1 adult to book 1 room, 2 adults to book 2 rooms, etc).
Price from GBP *£1,229.47*
First Class Double Room Code: FIRDBL First class double room. The number of adults selected corresponds to the number of double rooms requested (e.g. select 1 adult to book 1 room, 2 adults to book 2 rooms, etc).
Price from GBP *£1,765.39*

Additional Information:
Inclusions: Lima:
Round-trip arrival and departure transfers
(Day 1 and Day 8) Lima city tour
Two nights' accommodation in Lima
(Day 1 and Day 4). Hotel varies by option selected
Daily breakfast
Transfer to bus station for trip to Nazca
Bus ticket from Lima to Nazca (Day 2)
Transfer to airport to head to Cusco (Day 5)

Nazca:
Transfer from bus station to hotel (Day 2)
One night accommodation in Nazca (Day 2).
Hotel varies by option selected
Daily breakfast
Air tour over the Nazca Lines
Transfer from Nazca to Paracas (Day 3)

Paracas:
One night accommodation in Paracas (Day 3).
Hotel varies by option selected
Sightseeing cruise of the Ballestas Islands
Transfer from Paracas to Lima (Day 4)

Cusco:

Round-trip arrival and departure transfers (Day 5 and Day 8)
City tour:
Archaeological tour of Sacsayhuaman, Qengo, Puca Pucara and Tambomachay:
Transportation to and from train station in Cusco for trip to Machu Picchu
Roundtrip train tickets (Backpacker class)
Bus to and from the citadel of Machu Picchu from Aguas Calientes
Guided tour of Machu Picchu
Three nights' accommodation in Cusco (Day 5, 6 and 7).
Hotel varies by option selected
Daily breakfast

Exclusions:

Food and drinks unless specified
Gratuities (optional)
International airfare (to and from Peru)
Domestic airfare (round-trip to Cusco from Lima)
Airport taxes (USD$6.50 for domestic flights and USD$32.00 for international)

Additional Info:

Confirmation will be received at time of booking
Passport name, number, expiry and country are required at time of booking for all participants. Otherwise, your tour may not be confirmed.
When booking your domestic flight from Lima to Cusco, it must be in the morning. Arrival by noon is too late.
Upon time of booking, please provide flight itinerary for international flights and domestic flights

Please note: the number of adults selected corresponds to the number of rooms requested

Itinerary:

DAY 1 Upon arrival in Lima, you'll be met at the airport and taken directly to your hotel. In the afternoon, after you've rested a little, enjoy a Lima city tour to get you better acquainted with Peru's capital. Stroll through Lima's beautiful streets and plazas and soak in the sights of this historic city. You'll start at the Love Park in Miraflores district, with spectacular views of the Pacific Ocean. Then, make your way to San Isidro, the financial centre of the city, to visit Huaca Huallamarca, a famous pre-Incan shrine. After this, go on to the main square where the Government Palace and Town Hall are located. Visit Lima Cathedral and explore the San Francisco convent, which was built in the seventeenth century and is home to Lima's mysterious catacombs.

DAY 2

In the morning, you'll be picked up from your hotel and transferred to the bus station to depart to Nazca. Upon arrival, enjoy a welcoming reception and be transferred to your hotel. You'll have this evening free to explore the town or simply rest at the hotel.

DAY 3

In the morning, head to the local airfield to fly over the famous Nazca Lines in a private Cesna airplane! These huge geoglyphs, which represent several insects and animals, are best seen from the sky. The origins are unknown; many think it is a big astronomic calendar. In the afternoon, get on the bus and head to Paracas bay. Upon arrival, you'll be transferred to your hotel for an evening of leisure.

DAY 4

In the morning, embark on a scenic boat tour around the Ballesta Islands. One of the famous landmarks of this area of Peru is the famous Chandelier, a geoglyph which lies in the sand in the style of the Nazca Lines and is best seen from the water. On the islands, keep your eyes open for sea lions, pelicans, Humboldt penguins and other sea birds. In the afternoon, get back on the bus to transfer back to Lima.

DAY 5

In the morning, you'll be transferred to the airport for your flight to Cusco (flight is not included). It is highly recommended that you purchase tickets for a morning flight.
Upon arrival in Cusco, you'll be transferred to the hotel to freshen up before you begin exploring the mysterious city of Cusco. In the afternoon, your city tour begins with a visit to the San Cristobal.

Plaza, where you'll enjoy a panoramic view of the city. Then, visit the San Pedro Market to soak in its local flavours and to learn about more of the regional products that supply the whole city. Next, head over to the Korikancha temple and marvel at its magnificence. This temple, whose name in Quechua means "Gold Enclosure," will dazzle you with its gold-covered walls. Then, head over to Santo Domingo Church in the San Blas artisans' neighbourhood before heading to the Hatun Rumiyoc Street, making a stop at the Inca Roca Palace. Continue your walk to the main square to visit the Cathedral of Santo Domingo and admire its beautiful colonial masterpieces.

DAY 6

In the morning, you'll visit Sacsayhuaman, a huge fortress of colossal constructions and a true archaeological wonder. The adventure continues at the Inca shrine Qenqo, where you'll see a sacrificial altar embedded inside a rock cave. Finally, you'll arrive at the Puca Pucara viewpoint, home of the famous Tambomachay monument. You'll then have the afternoon free to explore the city on your own.

DAY 7

In the morning, board the train for a day at Machu Picchu! After your scenic journey on the train, you'll arrive at the Aguas Calientes station and board the bus to go up the winding road to Machu Picchu. Your visit is fully guided and your professional guide will answer any questions you have. After your visit, you'll have some free time to explore the fortress and have lunch at one of the restaurants in the area. Then take the train back to Cusco for your last night of the tour.

DAY 8

In the morning, you'll be transferred to the airport for your flight back to Lima.

Voucher Info: You must present a paper voucher for this tour. We will email a link to access and print your voucher at the Lead Travellers email address.

Local Operator Information: Complete Operator information, including local telephone numbers at your destination, are included on your Confirmation Voucher. Our Product Managers select only the most experienced and reliable operators in each destination, removing the guesswork for you, and ensuring your peace of mind. Since 1999, over 3 million travellers have experienced more with Viator!

Dear reader, the previous pages reflect my choice of itinerary. It was followed fairly accurately but with the exception of Day One. Due to the late arrival of the Manchester to Lima flight, I was obliged to miss out on the tour of Lima City. Instead I was taken directly to my hotel at Miraflores. But during the second week of my visit I was able to book a seat on a bus tour. It was one which enabled me to finally see the city. One last point to note is that the prices quoted in the previously mentioned itinerary can and probably will vary. Therefore please check with the tour operator for the latest pricing, before making any costing or plans to book a holiday.

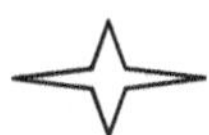

WHAT TO TAKE ON THE TRIP

From the outset I confess I had done a fair amount of travelling prior to this adventure. Nevertheless the holiday required careful planning. My previous experiences had taught me an important lesson. Before venturing on any journey make a list of all the items that are required. By doing this over the years I have managed to whittle down the list to a minimum. The idea being that the fewer items one packs the less weight one has to manage. Also the less there is to worry about. Of course, it naturally follows that the fewer items taken on a journey the smaller the suitcase needs to be.

My suitcase measures (Width) 36cm by (Length) 63cm by (Depth) 25cm. It has a pair of small wheels built into one end, which I consider to be essential for ease of mobility. A telescopic handle is incorporated at the opposite end which complements the arrangement. There are also two carrying handles. One attached to a long side and another to a short side. Both of which are designed for manoeuvring the case when those awkward situations occur. I find this particular design of suitcase to lend itself to the least amount of effort when handling.

As a means of identification, I tie a bright-orange plastic bag around one of the handles. It's nothing fancy, just an old supermarket shopping bag. But it helps me to spot my case more readily, when it is gliding along the airport carousel. Safe to say its usefulness outweighs any potential embarrassment it might cause me. The lid of the suitcase is held closed by the use of the integral zipper. This in turn is secured by using a small padlock. But fearing that the zipper might malfunction at some point in my journey and perhaps spill out its contents; I also employ the use of a fabric belt. It is taken from an old dressing gown and is tied around the belly of the suitcase.

It also serves as another recognisable feature when looking for it on the carousel. To the casual bystander the suitcase may have a certain 'refugee look' about it but at least it is safe and functional.

Having chosen my suitcase I ask the question; "What things do I need to take with me?" Apart from the usual clothing and personal toiletries perhaps the most important items to take are a passport and money.

PASSPORT

For any traveller it is advisable that a passport has a minimum of six months validity to satisfy the requirement of passport control. At the time of typing this information visitors to Peru from England don't require a visa or vaccination certificate but it is advisable to make sure before travelling.

The passport of course is NOT to be packed into a suitcase as it is required to be produced many times throughout the journey. It is also a good idea to make a photocopy of the page having the bearer's photograph on it and placed somewhere separate from the actual passport. In the unfortunate and hopefully unlikely event that the passport is lost, the photocopy may prove helpful when facing the authorities.

MONEY

The official currency of Peru is called the 'Nuevo Sol' although the local population refer to them simply as 'Soles'. The word Soles is the plural form of Sol and each Sol is made up of 100 centimos. The same principle applies in England where there are a hundred Pennies to the one Pound Sterling. Since Peru is relatively close to the U.S.A. the American Dollar is also readily accepted as currency. I found it to be a good idea to take some actual Soles with me on my trip.

Having a few Soles in one's pocket makes life easier on arrival to Peru. They ease the need to start hunting around for a currency exchange bureau. Also they are on hand to pay for that urgent taxi fare should the need arise. Besides having ready cash it is worthwhile taking a bank card for the odd emergency situation.

On one occasion when I was visiting the Peruvian city of Lima, I used my debit card at an ATM to draw some cash. To my amazement I found that the system actually worked. The instructions on the machine were printed in Spanish but the layout was the same as the ATM's in the UK. I quickly deciphered the relevant buttons and local currency was issued into my hand. After I returned home from my holiday I received the latest bank statement. Although I had withdrawn Soles from the ATM, the bank statement showed the equivalent amount in Sterling.

Traveller's cheques are another consideration but they have to be cashed when money is required. The finding of an exchange bureau can often prove difficult. But the benefit from using travellers' cheques is that they can be replaced if they are lost!

COMMISSION

Before closing the subject of money here are a few words of warning when it comes to exchanging Pounds for Soles. I found that most currency exchange dealers are making a profit at the conclusion of a monetary transaction. They call it 'commission.' This basically means they are charging a fee for the work that they do. It also helps to meet the costs of the overheads of running their business. However, beware of those that have a tendency to overcharge. Shop around for the best deal. Places to obtain currency are banks, post offices and even cash converter shops.

The latter tend to offer a better rate of exchange than the traditional institutions. Because their overheads are less they can afford to charge less. Try looking on the internet to locate the nearest branch to you. Quite often they operate an online service where you can pay for the required currency by bank card and have the travel cash actually delivered to your door.

Finally, beware of the places that say, 'Zero Commission' or 'No Commission Charged.' In my opinion they charge a higher exchange rate which in effect gives them the commission they desire.

In short, have a walk around to visit the three places mentioned. Suggest to the salesperson an amount, of say £300. Then ask how many Soles you can expect to get in your hand for that amount of British Pounds. I think that you will be surprised by comparing the results.

FROM MANCHESTER TO LIMA

****

My dream journey finally began on the third of June with a flight from Manchester Airport (U.K.) to Paris, France. Whilst crossing the airport tarmac to board the Paris flight, I mulled over what items I should have with me. A passport of course, was the first to remember and then keys and sun glasses came to mind. Suddenly my heart sank with deep despair! I realised that I had left my English bank notes at home. The ones I would exchange in case of a financial emergency. After all I wasn't to know if my bank card would work in Peru.

During those anxious moments I assured myself that it was too late to worry about them. Further assurance came from the thought that at least I did have some Peruvian Soles in my pocket. But then what if they weren't enough and what if my bank card wouldn't work? These questions could only be answered in due course. In the worst case scenario I would just have to ration my Soles until the end of the holiday.

Within a few minutes my mind turned the corner of despair and thought of an incident that made me smile. I once heard the story about an elderly couple. They were called Mr and Mrs Isaacs and like me, were flying from Manchester to Paris. Both stood in the queue waiting to pass through the security check. Mister Isaacs turned to his wife and said, "Rachel, I vish I hed brought de grand piano met us!"

She replied, "Vot do you vont met de grand piano, ve are only going to France?" With tears welling in his eyes the old man answered, "Because; I left the 'plane tickets on top of de grand piano!"

****

Try as I may I am unable to get accustomed to air travel. In terms of comfort it is never the best and yet here I was again, putting myself through the torment. On this occasion I was located close to the front of the aircraft. As I settled into a seat, my attention was drawn to two passengers and their conversation. One man said to the other, "Did you notice that there is no seat number thirteen? They number the seats that way for the sake of the superstitious!"

I had never considered the notion before and certainly never noticed the absence of seat number thirteen. However, having heard this revelation I made a concerted effort to look. Sure enough there was no seat number thirteen to be seen!

On any subsequent flight taken by me, I have always looked for that ominous number but it has always been missing. Is that strange or what?

Of course as one clever sage pointed out to me, there is still a seat that is technically number thirteen but it is not labelled as such!

As the pilot was preparing for takeoff, a flight steward stood in the aisle and demonstrated how to use a life jacket. On this particular flight, my seat location afforded a good view of the demo. I was able to take a close look at the actual life jacket. Printed on the fabric I noticed some small lettered words. They said, 'DUNMURRAY BELFAST NORTHERN IRELAND'.

The thought occurred to me that 'Dunmurray' must be the company that manufactured the life jacket. Then I remembered that Belfast was the place where the ocean liner, RMS Titanic, was built. I suddenly realised that the aircraft would soon be flying over the Atlantic Ocean. In all probability it might fly over or perhaps close to the route taken by the ill-fated ship. The life jacket suddenly seemed quite appropriate!

The twelve and a half hour flight from Paris to Lima was far too long for my liking. However, some little consolation was to be had from the fact that it was a daytime flight. As such there was lots of activity taking place. Various people moved about from time to time. Foodstuffs and drinks were served at what seemed like regular intervals. I also got my first look at some Peruvian people. I think they made up about 90% of the passengers. They seemed to be a friendly bunch and had a distinctive look about them. It was one that set them aside from Europeans. They had beige coloured skin and mostly black hair, although I did see a blonde or two amongst them. All were seemingly of a uniform height of around five feet six inches.

As the 'plane approached Peru it commenced its descent in readiness for landing. Fear began to grip me. It wasn't fear stemming from the thought of landing. It was the thought that the tour people might not be waiting for me!

Lima airport, compared to that of Manchester, is smaller but modern. Contrary to the reports I had heard, the service and amenities offered by the Peruvian Airways, was quite efficient.

It wasn't long before I was standing next to a carousel and waiting for my suitcase to arrive. I watched the conglomeration of baggage as it travelled seemingly endlessly along. It appeared to float like pieces of flotsam on some ocean waves. Suddenly an example of Peruvian security manifested itself. It took the form of drug seeking policemen with sniffer dogs. They jumped up alongside the carousel and sniffed the suitcases as they moved along. I hasten to add it was the dogs that sniffed the baggage and not the policemen!

I caught sight of my case with its orange plastic bag and pleased to say it arrived unchallenged by neither man or beast.

Making my way to the exit door I was delighted to see a group of officials lined up. They were waiting to greet the arriving passengers. Some carried small boards, on which was written the name of the person they were to collect. Thankfully mine was amongst them.

Introductions were exchanged and my identifying tour voucher was inspected. The Viator guides drove swiftly towards what was to be the first hotel of my tour.

The holiday itinerary stated that after my arrival I would be whisked away to the City centre. There I would be shown the famous sights. Unfortunately, because of the late arrival, that part of the tour was waivered. At least for the time being.

As our little party travelled along, the informative driver brought to my attention the colour of the afternoon sky. He declared that, "Off the coast of Lima a spreading mist is produced. It rises and forms a grey blanket, which hangs in the sky for the most part of the day. It is caused by a warm current of water that mixes with the sea. Because of this phenomenon the locals refer to the city as 'Lima the grey'."

Having spent twelve and a half hours in an aeroplane, whilst hoping to escape the grey sky of Manchester, this revelation came as something of a shock. Fortunately however, the next morning I was due to leave Lima and travel south to sunnier climes.

At first glance the Hotel el Tambo looked more like a house than a hotel. It was one of a row of properties in a street that all looked very much alike. They were modern concrete and brick structures of two storeys in height and were surrounded by security walls. Actually the hotel is located in a district of Lima called Miraflores, which is about a twenty minute taxi ride outside the city centre.

By all accounts Miraflores is considered to be perhaps the safest suburb of all and is favoured by locals and tourists alike. It offers a varied choice of shops and restaurants and places of interest. Security is ever present in Peru and something that simply becomes part of everyday life.

After checking in to the hotel I walked along the streets to familiarise myself with the central part of the suburb. My first impression was that of the climate. The time was 2100hrs and the ambient temperature was still noticeably warm. If anything the air was humid but it felt wonderful! The area was teeming with people and traffic, all of which were going somewhere but I had no idea where! Perhaps like me they were looking for somewhere to eat.

I had been warned about buying food from roadside vendors which by doing so I ran the risk of food poisoning. To my surprise I suddenly saw a MacDonald's food outlet and instantly felt at ease. The food shop offered polite and good humoured service, something that I found endemic to Peru. Some minutes later I walked from the shop carrying the biggest cheese burger I had ever eaten. Together with potato frites and a coke drink, I paid 16 Soles for the lot. On reflection the price was perhaps a tad expensive. But at that early stage of my tour it didn't faze me too much.

Nearby was a popular parkland. It was there I found a vacant bench on which to sit and quietly consume my food. The park was divided into two areas with the largest known as Central Park, whilst the smaller was called Kennedy Park. It was at Kennedy Park where I was destined to spend a lot of time in the days to come. During the 1980's the parkland was infested by numerous rodents and so cats were introduced with a view to reducing their population.

The cats ultimately triumphed over the vermin and now there are around fifty to eighty that are looked after by the municipality. The Park is cleaned on a daily basis and any smells or droppings produced by the cats are safely taken away. In its entirety the park is like the beating heart of Miraflores. It provides a venue for a mix of visitors and vendors of various kinds. There are a number of food outlets of which some are small one-man enterprises, whilst others are medium sized restaurants.

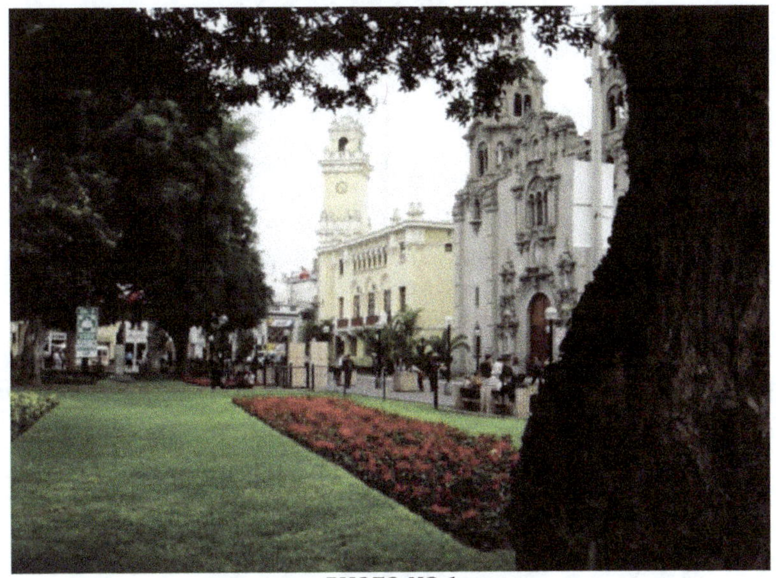

PHOTO NO 1
A SECTION OF KENNEDY PARK

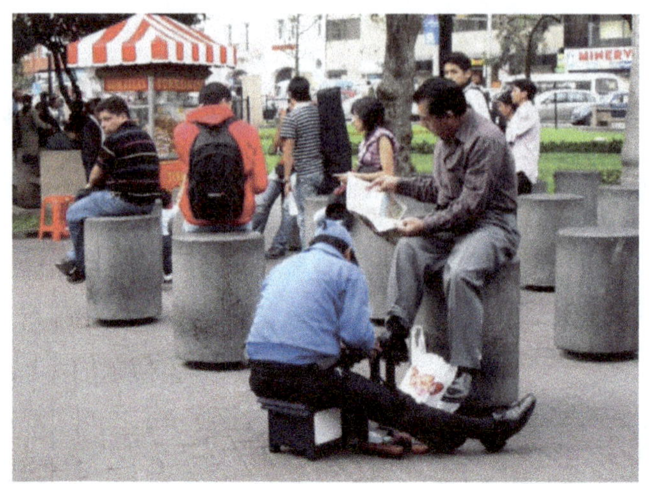

PHOTO NO 2
A SHOESHINE MAN AT WORK IN KENNEDY PARK

Shoeshine men are to be readily found and appear to conduct a brisk trade. Since I was on holiday, I decided to experience the relative luxury of having someone actually clean and polish my shoes. Imagining myself to be a millionaire, I sat and watched a shoeshine man, as he deftly transformed my travel-weary shoes into a sight to behold.

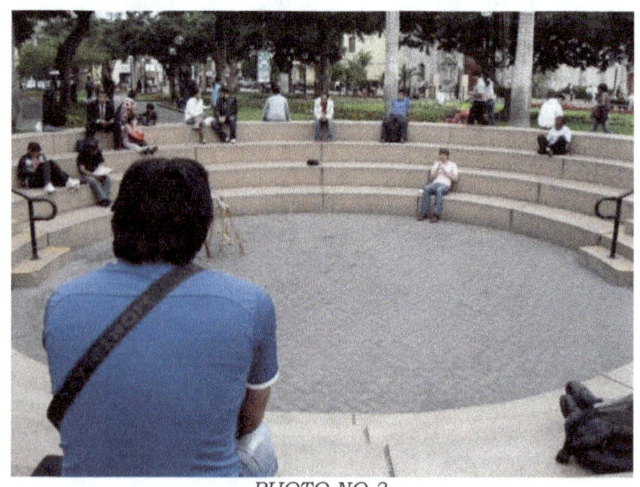

PHOTO NO 3
THE AMPHITHEATRE AT KENNEDY PARK

At one section of the park there is a circular concrete amphitheatre. It measures about thirty feet in diameter and incorporates tiered seating. During the day the casual visitor may sit on the steps to rest or to chat to a friend. But as night-time arrives it becomes a vibrant family affair. The family unit appears to be one of the notable characteristics of the Peruvian society. All genders and all ages gather to witness or to take part in some form of entertainment. An impromptu band might casually strike up and play a musical rendition of a waltz. The more senior members of the gathering are then at liberty to pair off. Thereafter they may be seen to gleefully shuffle around the floor space. On another evening more up-beat forms of music might be created. It is then when the younger people have a chance to show off their dancing, or even singing skills!

After buying the MacDonald's burger it occurred to me that it might be prudent to test the local ATM outlets. If there were any potential problems they could be sorted out sooner, rather than later. I quickly spotted a familiar cash outlet but was slightly off put by the operating instructions. They were printed in Spanish. This was hardly surprising considering the country I was in! But in all honesty I thought that in view of the many foreign visitors that frequent the city, they might have had dual instructions. The second set in English of course! Fortunately the format of the instructions and layout of the key board were more or less the same as the European equivalent. Because of this it wasn't too much of a problem to translate the wording and to complete the transaction. Very soon I was richer in pocket. I also felt more at ease, knowing that should I need extra cash in the future, the system did in fact work.

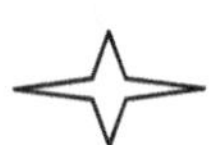

FROM LIMA TO NAZCA

****

I slept soundly during my first night spent in Miraflores and awoke the next morning feeling refreshed and ready for action. A basic but wholesome breakfast was provided at the hotel. It comprised of freshly baked bread rolls with slices of cooked meat and slices of cheese. Fruit juice, tea and coffee were also available together with freshly made fruit salad. I soon learned to eat enough food to keep me 'going' for most of the day. I also made a sandwich, discreetly of course, to keep in my camera bag for an emergency snack. With the amount of travelling I had to do, meal times were not always predictable, so it was advisable to be prepared.

After re-packing my suitcase I took it to the hotel's reception area. From there I didn't have long to wait before transport arrived. Two trusty guides took me to an Expreso Cruz del Sur bus station. It was a few minutes drive from Miraflores and located on the edge of the two municipal districts of La Victoria and San Isidro. According to the Expreso Cruz del Sur bus company, it has been transporting passengers on the roads and highways of Peru, for more than forty-two years. It is also considered to be the leader in its field. [3] At the station I was to board a bus that would take me to Nazca. (Nasca) Once there I was pre-booked to fly in a light aircraft and over the famous Nazca Lines. The lines consist of numerous ancient markings that are etched into the desert surface. Their purpose has long been shrouded in mystery.

On my arrival to the bus station it was bustling with people coming from and going to various destinations in Peru. A long desk occupied a wall that served as the inquiry centre and also the place from where to purchase travel tickets.

Adorning the wall immediately behind the desk was a large map showing the entire coastline of Peru. Numerous dots were printed along its length and each was labelled with a place name. Presumably the map illustrated the extensive route that was serviced by the bus company.

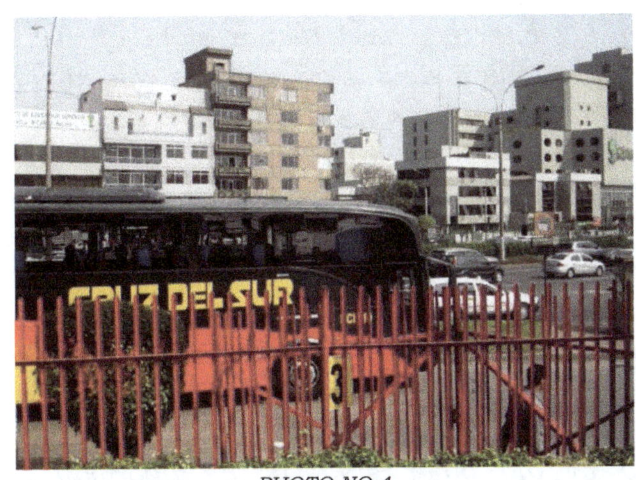

PHOTO NO 4

TOUR BUS BOUND FOR NAZCA - NOTE THE HIGH POSITIONED PASSENGER SEATS ALSO THE SECURITY FENCING AROUND THE BUS STATION

Also the 'dots' represented the places that could be visited by any potential traveller. Meanwhile, as one of the guides was purchasing my bus ticket, I looked around the immediate waiting area. Bench seats were provided for the use of the commuters, who waited patiently for their respective bus to arrive. There was a television monitor that was fixed to a wall. It was just high enough to be out of reach from meddling fingers. The monitor was showing live coverage of a national football match; the like of which the average Peruvian enjoys. Clutching my newly purchased bus ticket, I deposited my suitcase at a nearby security desk. It was exchanged for a second ticket that would allow me to retrieve the item once I had reached my destination.

At 1320hrs, just ten minutes before the departure time, a man arrived wearing a two-piece suit. He calmly took up a stance behind a free standing lectern. A security badge pinned to a lapel of his jacket, was the only clue that indicated he was an official employee. He shuffled a few papers on top of the lectern and then looked up to see who was in the queue.

About the same time and within sight of everyone, a beautifully painted double-decker bus glided to a halt. Minutes later, the man, who acting like some musical conductor, waved his arm to indicate he was ready. Since I was the first in line I stepped briskly forward and proffered my passport, together with the bus ticket. After exchanging cordial greetings, the man scrutinised my documents. Acknowledging that they were in order, he gesticulated that I should move through a doorway that gave access to the bus. Both were less than two metres away.

Waiting at the other side of the doorway stood a uniformed security guard. He politely requested to look at my passport. Whilst holding a miniature metal detector he stroked it over my camera bag and then myself. His curiosity was satisfied and accepting that I was no terrorist, he directed me towards the front of the parked bus. Walking along its length brought me face to face with both the uniformed driver and a conductor. Their friendly greeting began with "Buenos dias" (Good Day) and then, surprisingly, I was politely asked to show them my passport and bus ticket!! There could be no doubting that security was tops in this place. Before leaving the U.K., I read that in the past, the occasional bus had been shot at from the hills or even hijacked. Clearly these people were concerned for the safety of their passengers. Whilst returning my documents the conductor directed me towards a seat that was located on the upper deck and at the same time wished me a pleasant journey. The bus seats and tickets were numbered, which meant there was no confusion about seating arrangements. I was obliged to sit where I had been allocated, which as it happened, was a good choice. The seat was particularly comfortable, having the usual function of being able to recline but with the addition of an adjustable leg rest.

Just as the last passenger was seated, the security guard appeared at the top of the stairs. He was the one who had previously screened me with his metal detector. This time he was brandishing a camcorder. He quietly and quickly proceeded to record each person whilst they remained seated. I later learned that this was a measure to counter-act terrorism. The thought being that a potential terrorist might plan to board the bus and choose to strike later, during the journey. That being the case the authorities at least had a visual image of the culprit. Not such a bad idea when considering the times in which we presently live.

Surprisingly the bus departed on time and slowly edged its way out of the terminus and on to the main road. Safety was clearly a consideration on this trip and was further emphasised when an overhead television monitor burst into life. It began showing a pre-recorded video that explained aspects of travel safety.

A virtual attendant explained how to fasten one's seat belt. It also explained where the on board toilets were situated. I gleaned that there was a toilet located on both the upper and lower decks. "How very convenient" I thought. (Pardon the pun!)

Unfortunately one piece of video information gave me cause for concern. It was the advice that passengers should draw the curtain across the viewing window, that was located next to their seat.

I presume this was intended to prevent any potential assailant from seeing who was on board. After careful consideration I decided to run the risk. My fascination for the changing scenery outside the bus and the desire to see as much of the country as possible, overcame any thought of my being eradicated by a sniper's bullet!

When the video ended the conductor re-appeared. He made sure everyone was wearing their seat belt and handed out a small pillow and a blanket. They were hygienically sealed in plastic bags. I instantly felt like I was going to enjoy my journey. That is, if I could just manage to open the stubborn plastic bags!

****

From time to time throughout the journey, the conductor asked each passenger if anything was required. A small meal and a cool drink were provided with the cost of the bus ticket. Extra refreshments came at a price.

The time was 2130hrs when the bus finally arrived in the town of Nazca. The journey had taken a full eight hours! During that time I had merely sat and enjoyed the passing views. But as I stepped down from the bus I was feeling not only travel weary but also rather peckish.

As if by acting on some invisible cue, a waiting tour guide stepped forward and introduced himself.

He was a young man named Raul, who was designated to drive me to a hotel. His somewhat less than perfect, gas-propelled car, was our mode of transport. The hotel at which I was to spend the night was named Casa Andina Classic. Its website described it as: 'Combining traditional Andean décor and an urban feel, with modern facilities. Casa Andina offers an outdoor swimming pool and free WIFI and is just one block from Nazca's historic main square.'[4]

At the hotel I put my suitcase into a basic but nonetheless adequate room and then I joined Raul. He had volunteered to show me his favourite local restaurant. By this time my stomach was making rumbling sounds. We walked along the main street that was pulsating with activity. People young and old were taking in the evening air and the traffic was fairly active. Taking care to avoid the cars, we crossed the street to enter a large house. It had been converted into an eating place. At the entrance stood an armed security guard. The sight of which reminded me of the time I had spent in South Africa.

During the latter part of the Apartheid era there was a lot of violent crime in Johannesburg. As a result many restaurants thought it prudent to employ a marksman to protect their customers. Perhaps parts of Peru had experienced outbursts of criminality and therefore prevention was thought to be better than cure. I tried not to think about any possible danger and proceeded to enjoy the moment.

The restaurant teetered on the edge of austerity. It had bare wooden floors, with wooden tables and matching chairs. All the frills of a modern restaurant were not to be seen here. But the place gave off a pleasant vibration that mingled with the gentle buzz of the diners. Along the length of a wall was a cooking range that had the facility to roast chickens and fry potato chips. There was also a section where one could buy take-a-way food, which included burgers and even freshly baked cakes. Here was my opportunity to learn something of the Spanish language. I soon understood that 'Pollo con papa frites' translated into English means 'chicken with chips'. After a day or two of snacking on hotel buffets and bus transport snacks, the chicken and fried chipped potatoes tasted like ambrosia to me!

During the meal Raul explained that he lived with his brother and their parents. They shared a modest house that was located in Nazca. He revealed that his family, with the exception of his father, practised the Roman Catholic faith. I understood that almost 75% of Peru's population did likewise. This information didn't surprise me but what he told me next most certainly did!

He confessed that at his home the family were tormented by the presence of a malevolent spirit, or in other words a poltergeist! His brother was particularly troubled because the spirit actually pushed him about. Raul was obviously concerned by the situation. I was surprised that he should take me into his confidence but at the same time I felt privileged that he did.

I was no expert in such matters but I did know a verse or two from the Holy Bible, which I shared with him. I suggested that he and his family speak the verses audibly inside their home, in an attempt to get the spirit to move away.

His predicament caused me to express my concern. "Surely", I said, "There must be someone living in Nazca, who would have the knowledge to rid the house of its unwanted entity?" Time would prove to be my judge.

Our conversation drifted towards the subject of the Nazca Lines, which I planned to visit the next day. Hopefully I would take an aeroplane flight to view them from the air. According to all accounts, after Machu Picchu the 'Lines' are Peru's second most important tourist attraction. Their existence was largely unknown until the first half of the 20th century. It was aviators busy fumigating the cotton fields in the valley, who saw them for the first time from the air. Furthermore, their designs only became known to the scientific community in the late 1930's. One suggestion for their use is that they form the world's largest astronomical calendar.

Another purport is that they point in the direction of fertile valleys or river basins. [5] Both seem like valuable considerations in such a markedly arid environment.

Raul was well informed about the local places of interest. Besides telling me about the Nazca Lines, he happened to mention the ancient pyramids of Cahuachi. They stood within a few miles from the Nazca Lines. "What, Pyramids in Peru?" I questioned; "How could that be possible?" He described them as being large pyramid shaped mounds that were constructed using adobes; or put more simply, mud bricks!

Estimated to have been in use between 450BC and 450AD they are located in the desert area between Nazca and the Pacific Ocean. Furthermore, it was suggested that the priesthood of the ancient Nazca people lived there and possibly practised human sacrifice. I flippantly remarked, "I wonder if the priests ever got it perfect!"

Nearly thirty years of excavation and research by the Italian mission, led by archaeologist Giuseppe Orefici, have uncovered what was the epicentre of the Nazca culture. A large temple is viewable in a complex that was previously covered by sand and mud. I was intrigued by this revelation and my immediate question was; "What would it take for me to see them?" Raul was very obliging. He made a quick 'phone call to the tour people and came up with a costing but there was a proviso. A rough calculation estimated that we should have to leave my hotel by no later than 0630hrs. By so doing, it would be possible to visit the pyramids and also for me to be at the airfield in time for the flight. The temptation was too great. I willingly agreed although I didn't sleep much that night for fear of being late!

****

THE CAHUACHI PYRAMIDS

****

On the morning of June the fifth I got to the hotel dining room with the hope of having an early breakfast. Luckily for me the entrance door was unlocked. Without hesitation I quickly drank a cup of tea. Stealthily I prepared a couple of cheese and meat sandwiches to take on my journey. Raul arrived on time and long before the sun made an appearance in the sky, we were on our way. We stopped briefly at a petrol station to buy fuel for his car. In this case the car used low pressure gas.

Throughout my visit to Peru I noticed it was common for cars to be fitted with a specially designed gas tank. It was located inside the boot compartment. The extra mileage gained by using low pressure gas, made the conversion from petrol all the more worthwhile.

As the car was being re-fuelled I asked the attendant if he knew of anyone who could rid Raul's house of the unwanted spirit. I realised this was an unusual request. But I reasoned that since the filling station was central to the area and the only one for many miles, the attendant must know lots of people. He looked bewildered by my inquiry. Raul spoke fluent Spanish to clarify the request but there was no positive response. "Never mind" said I reassuringly, "I feel convinced that someone in this vastly populated region, will be able to help you."

****

The sun was low in the sky as we approached Cahuachi. The Nazca people of long ago gave it its name which means 'From where you look.' It is considered to be the world's largest ceremonial site and covers some twenty-four square kilometres. According to Peruvian historian, Josue Lancho Rojas, the place is spiritually connected with the Nazca Lines. He claims that the high priests of Cahuachi, led the people from the pyramids and on to where the Nazca lines are constructed. They then carried out religious ceremonies.

At Cahuachi there are 36 known pyramids ranging between 15 metres (49 feet) and 35 metres (115 feet) in height. The main structure is known as the 'Grand Pyramid' and measures 28 metres (92 feet) in height, by 110 metres (361 feet) in length and 100 metres (328 feet) in width. The unique structure of this pyramid includes seven levels, having adobe walls and geometric access ramps. [6]

That is the official description of Cahuachi but the following describes the writer's personal observation.

At the point of leaving the main tarred road, on the outskirts of Nazca, I noticed what looked like a makeshift factory. It stood at the foot of a nearby hill with large piles of strange looking material stacked on the ground. It transpired that the factory's function was to process the 'strange piles.' They just happened to be seaweed! The produce is used as food for animals and I believe as an ingredient in certain medicines.

Raul and I travelled along the compacted-soil road, which wound its way through the desert terrain. The route was marked by dubious looking, short wooden sticks, that were stuck into the ground at irregular intervals. But their apparent look of impermanence caused me some concern. Raul assured me that he actually knew the route. He said he had driven along it many times before. My troubled mind was finally put at rest when the pyramids eventually came into view.

Essentially, to me they looked like rolling hills or sand dunes if you like. They were strung out over a wide area, rather like a necklace of beads. The ground on which the pyramids stand is desert terrain, which consists of coarse grainy soil that is beige in colour and contains a large proportion of miniature stones. The shape of the hills roughly resemble that of the famous Egyptian pyramids. Although, they have rounded tops and are much less than their original height. Having said that they do provide a natural base upon which to construct terraces, having walls and rooms and all made from mud-adobes. Collectively they present an impressive sight and are undoubtedly worth the effort to view them.

A few minutes had been consumed from our limited time. The sun had risen some distance above the horizon, causing dark shadows to be cast across the surface of the Grand Pyramid. Without us realising, it had morphed into a place suggesting it might still be occupied. Had the people and priests who had lived there centuries ago returned to haunt us?. But there was a tangible sense of stillness that pervaded the site; even though a gentle breeze blew in from the distant Pacific Ocean.

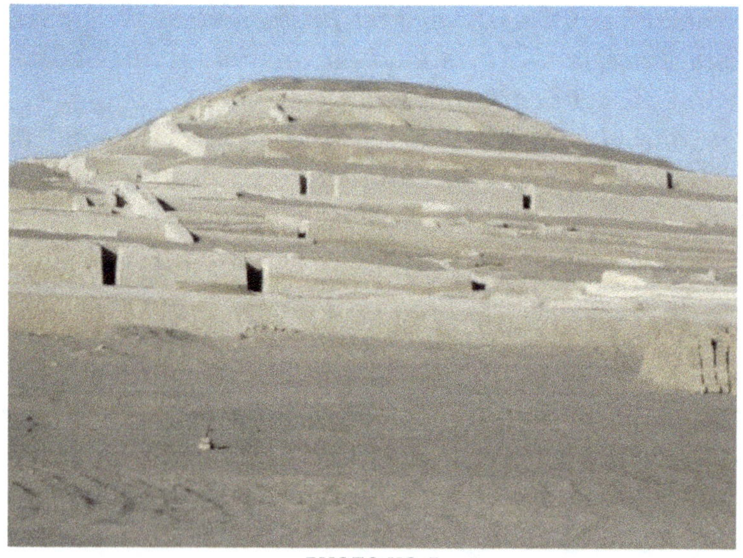

PHOTO NO 5
A VIEW OF THE GRAND PYRAMID OF CAHUACHI

A short climb up a soil-made ramp took me to the top of a smaller pyramid. From there I could observe the surrounding area and look across the expanse of open ground. In full view was the magnificent 'Grand Pyramid.' It stood in stark contrast to the backdrop of a blue tinted Peruvian sky.

Cahuachi existed for eight centuries and played host to large numbers of pilgrims from the surrounding valleys. They gathered to take part in various rituals. Following this period the city was abandoned. Its outer walls were demolished and the many pyramids were buried beneath the sands. From then onwards they ceased to pose as artificial monuments and returned to nature as towering sandy hills. From this site it is a short distance along the valley and over the hills to the desert plain. There the famous Nazca Lines and geometric patterns are to be seen.

Could the rituals carried out at Cahuachi and those performed at the Nazca Lines be part of the same mass gatherings? The answer remains to be seen.

A small wooden hut housed a watchman, who was employed to guard the site against trespassers. Prior to our departure Raul entered the hut. He spent a few moments thanking the guard for allowing us to visit. Curiously though it seemed, the watchman had remained out of sight during the whole of the time that we were there.

As we departed I glanced at my watch and realised there was still time to spare before my Nazca flight. Suddenly, I remembered some ancient stone aqueducts at Cantalloc and Ocongalla, which Raul had previously mentioned. Predictably, I casually inquired if we might view them.

****

CANTALLOC AND OCONGALLA

Located in the valley near to Nazca are over a hundred aqueducts. They were built to convey water from its source in the Andes mountain range and to the area. Raul and I visited the most important of these that are situated at Cantalloc and Ocongalla.

In terms of Peruvian history, it was the Nazca people, dating from the pre-Hispanic period, who discovered the subterranean water sources. They developed a system of ducts, which utilized the natural slope of the land, to channel the water from a higher point.

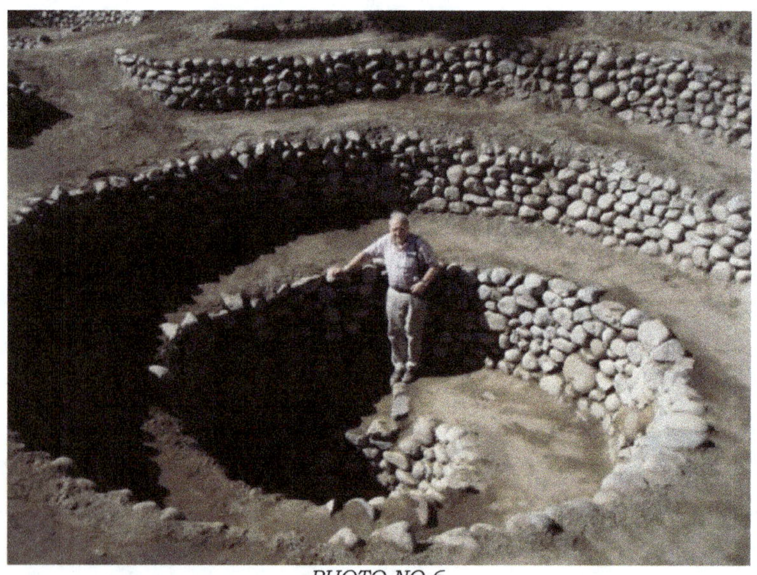

PHOTO NO 6
THE AUTHOR PICTURED ABOVE A SUBTERRANEAN CHANNEL WHICH
CONVEYS AIR-COOLED WATER TO THE SURROUNDING AREA

Flowing along subterranean ducts the water would surface periodically at lower points along the natural gradient. By using this method, the Nazca people were able to irrigate the desert and thereby create a prospering community. The side walls of the aqueducts were strengthened by using closely-fitted stones and then covered with stone slabs, or sometimes slices of hard wood. The Nazca engineers took their project a step further in their quest for perfection. They built spiral-like structures at regular intervals along the route. The spirals were made wide enough to walk down their path-like design, in order to facilitate maintenance of the ducts. [7] Raul explained to me another facet of the design. He said the spiral shape promotes an air vortex, that permeates the flowing water and thereby acts as a cooling agent.

A LOOK AT EL TELAR

There was an unexpected bonus that was attached to the aqueduct visit. It came in the form of a section of the Nazca Lines. These were known to the locals as 'El Telar.' Raul parked his car next to a small hill and to the top of which we slowly climbed. From its summit there was a commanding view of an open desert. In the distance stood mountains that poked majestically into the sky. Beyond them and just visible above the skyline was the famous Cerro Blanco. The lines appeared to point in its direction.

Cerro Blanco is the name given to what is considered to be the tallest sand dune in the world. If the reader looks carefully at the following photograph of El Telar (Photo No7) the peak of the sand dune can just be seen on the top left of the sky line.

The lines of El Telar look like a three-lane highway that merge into one. They stretch for a couple of miles in an easterly direction and towards the mountain range. It is believed that the mountains held some spiritual significance for the Nazca people.

Being overcome by the excitement of the occasion, I scrambled down the hill and actually stood on the Nazca Lines. What a joy! Looking over the ground I pondered as to how the ancients had constructed them.

By chance I noticed many fragments of broken ceramics, that were strewn about the surface. When I mentioned them to Raul he confirmed they had probably been there for hundreds of years. Perhaps as part of a ritual, designed to promote the provision of rain water, ceramic vessels containing gifts for the gods, may well have been brought to this site and broken.

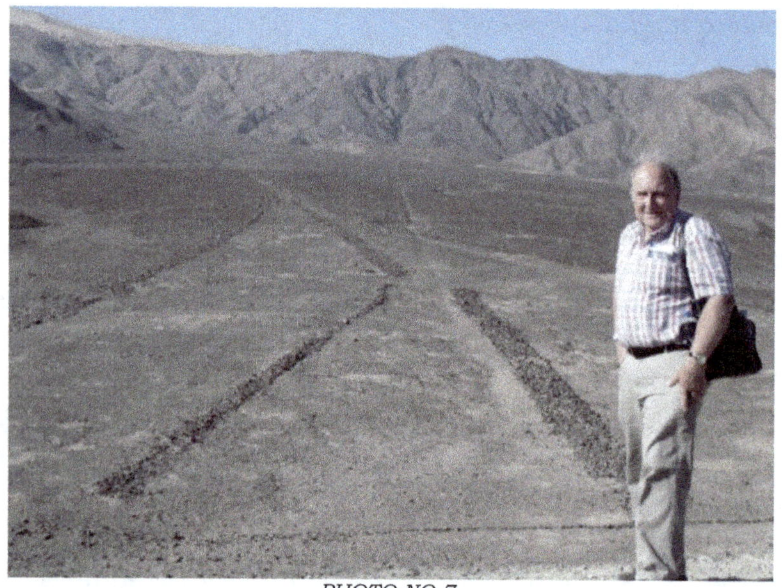

PHOTO NO 7
THE AUTHOR STANDING NEXT TO EL TELAR WITH CERRO BLANCO POKING ABOVE THE MOUNTAIN RANGE IN THE TOP LEFT HAND CORNER

Time seemed to pass quickly and we were on our way to keep my appointment with an aeroplane. It was one that I hoped would safely fly me over the Nazca Lines.

THE NAZCA AIRPORT

The journey to the airport was interrupted by a brief stop at a hotel. We collected an English tourist who was named Kenneth. He also wanted to take a flip in a Nazca aeroplane. I soon learned he had journeyed from the U.K. to South America by ship.

Arriving at Argentina he had disembarked in Buenos Aries. Having transported his motor bike across the Atlantic Ocean he rode it overland to Lima. Aged somewhere in his mid-fifties, he realized he was not getting any younger. Since his family were provided for, he took the proverbial bull by the horns and ventured forth. His wife had declined the offer to join him. How amazing; and I thought I was adventurous! My desire to quiz him further was unfortunately thwarted by our arrival at the airport.

This was nothing like any previous airport I had seen. It was small and unpretentious but nonetheless it had the amenities that anyone might want. These included toilets and a refreshment area. But I'm not sure which was the larger of the two! The fleet of aircraft were parked on the nearby tarmac. But a security barrier prevented anyone from leaving the single storey building.

Gazing through the windows of the mini departure lounge, I could clearly see a single engine Cessna 208. It was waiting to carry me over the mysterious Lines. At this moment I was feeling a tinge of apprehension. It was brought on by what I had previously read. There had been fatalities resulting from poorly maintained aircraft. They had flown from this very same airfield. In particular there was one when four Britons were killed as recently as October 2010! [8]

I assured myself that the present aircraft looked quite modern and that the Peruvian Government had intervened in recent years. It ensured that all aircraft flown from this airport were maintained to a high standard. (No pun intended!)

A voice hailed me and I was ushered towards a reception desk. My passport and flight ticket were scrutinized. The flight ticket was exchanged for a 'Boarding Pass' which was printed with the flight details along with my name.

What it also showed was my seat number, which as the reader shall see, was to be most relevant later that morning.

Afterwards I was directed to another desk, where I was obliged to pay an airport tax amounting to 25 Soles. In exchange for my money I received a brightly printed ticket that displayed the following words:

Ticket for the using of the airport Maria Reiche: Installation from district Vista Allegre: Nazca: Tax Included: Medical Services: Toilet Services: Tourist Information: Assistance.

Considering the list of things that were provided and all for the sum of 25 Soles, I tend to think that was good value for money. I had of course paid for the aeroplane flight but that was included with the cost of the tour.

Incidentally, Maria Reiche, whose name was printed on my ticket, was a German born mathematician and archaeologist. She had spent years of her life researching the Nazca Lines.

In addition to the parallel lines, she saw there were also eighteen different shapes of animals and birds. They were all etched into the desert surface. Her theory was that the creators of the lines used them as a sun calendar and an observatory for astronomical cycles. Today it is widely believed that they were used for religious ceremonies, related to the calling of water from the gods. [9] In recognition of Maria Reiche's research the airport is named after her.

Carrying my official Boarding Pass, I followed a group of people. They walked through a monitored security gate and into the late morning sunshine. We headed towards a twelve seated Cessna aircraft, which was parked on the runway. I sat on the first available seat and was just about to fasten a seat belt when a female voice rang out. "You're sitting in my seat!"

Taken aback I looked at my Boarding Pass. A seat number was printed on its face but I hadn't seen any numbers on the seats. "Well, where is mine then?" I retorted. An unrelated passenger pointed to my allocated seat. Miraculously the back of each seat was suddenly printed with a number! Why hadn't I noticed them earlier? Guess who felt embarrassed?

My choice of seat was on the starboard side but now I was directed to the port side. Because of this I felt somewhat cheated. Later in the morning my disappointment was ratified. For the most part, the 'plane banked to the starboard and it became evident that the best views were in fact on that side. But in spite of all of this it was an enjoyable flight.

Before the flight people recalled that their plane had bobbed and weaved due to air pockets. But contrary to these reports, for me the trip was smooth and uneventful. Although, in my opinion the aircraft flew too high. It made it difficult to recognize some of the more notable shapes etched on the desert plain. Also it didn't help the situation when the pilot spoke little English. For most of the flight he gave the commentary in Spanish. But the names of the most famous shapes, such as the 'Condor' or the 'Spider,' I was able to understood.

According to local legend the 'Spider' represents fertility and water. In respect to the water, it is said that the spider was seen to appear at a time when rain was about to fall, or when rivers were about to rise. The shape of a 'Monkey' was another that I recognised. I am told that it measures 90 metres in length and shows one of its hands as having five fingers, whilst the other has only four. Evidently the sum of the fingers represents the number of months of drought that the Nazca people suffered each year. Sometimes a shape was indiscernible from the sky, or at least from where I was sitting. However, I clearly saw the 'Humming bird' and the 'Heron bird' and also the shape known as the 'Astronaut'.

According to researcher Maria Reiche the humming bird is associated with the summer solstice. Her idea is that one of the lines connected to the bird's beak, points towards the place where the sun rises every year, during the summer solstice. Unlike the other shapes, the astronaut is etched on the slope of a small hill and not on the horizontal desert surface. Also, his body is facing to the south.

Paradoxically Maria Reiche maintains that the shape does not represent an astronaut, but rather a shaman or ancient Nazca priest. He was a person having magical powers and who could predict the weather.

What impressed me most about the Lines was the number and length of them and the fact that they range over nearly 200 square miles. They are of course best seen from the air; as one can appreciate the size and extent of the lines in one look.

The depictions of lines and figures have been produced by relocating stones. They have been picked up from the surface of the desert plain and then put into a fresh position. The exposed ground from beneath the stones is lighter in colour, since prior to exposure it has not been subjected to rain or sunshine. Whilst on the other hand, the disturbed stones have a weathered patina which contrasts with the newly exposed ground. Thus the lines and shapes are created.

During her research Maria Reiche found evidence left by the creators. It suggested that they had used a combination of handmade rope and wooden stakes to act as guides when making the straight lines.

The flying time lasted for around twenty minutes before the aeroplane made its way back to the airfield.

On the return journey the pilot announced that in the distance, about nine miles east of Nazca, could be seen a carpet of brown coloured mountains. Beyond them were actual sand dunes that consisted of brightly coloured sand. One dune in particular stood high above the line of the brown mountains. It is called the 'Cerro Blanco' or the 'White Mountain' and has the honour of being the highest sand dune in the world! It has also been described as the 'Everest of the desert and mother of all dunes.' [10]

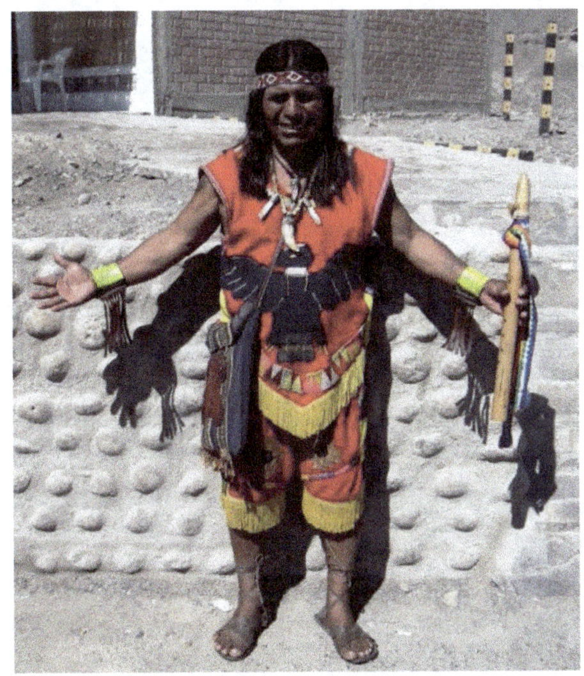

PHOTO NO 8
A PERUVIAN SHAMAN WEARING TRADITIONAL DRESS

Before the flight I noticed a man wearing the traditional dress of the ancient Nazca people. He was standing near the boarding gate with no apparent purpose, other than to chat to any inquiring tourist. Such was my understanding but I later found that he offered much more.

His long black hair was held back from his face by a patterned bandana and his main item of clothing was a poncho type garment. It had been woven from bright red cloth and was edged with yellow tassels. Blazoned across the front of the poncho and in stark contrast to the red cloth, was the image of a large black bird. The bird was more than likely to be a condor!

A coloured fabric bag hung loosely from a shoulder, whilst underneath the poncho, he wore a pair of matching breeches that reached down to his knees. To add a finishing touch to his apparel he wore brightly coloured wrist bands. They looked similar to the ones worn by tennis players. Around his neck hung a beaded necklace, attached to which were items that resembled the teeth of a large animal.

I had wanted to make a photograph of this colourful subject before the flight but it wasn't possible. Now that the flight was over and the man was still available I decided to 'capture' him. Whilst explaining to Raul what I was about to do he casually mentioned that the man was a local shaman. "What did you say?" I exclaimed. Raul repeated that the man was a shaman and to be sure that I understood he said, "He is a spiritual man."

"That's it!" I cried, "That's who we need to speak to. He has got to be the one who can rid you of your malevolent spirit!" I continued to explain that if we were to speak with this man and describe the problem, I felt sure he would be able to help.

Following a three-way dialogue the shaman became aware of Raul's predicament and announced that he could indeed offer assistance. He even recalled examples of people he had helped in the past. Raul's eyes stared widely as he slowly became convinced that the man would be able to assist him. With that assurance, the two of them agreed to meet at a future date.

By this time I was feeling elated. This was the one man who lived in the area and who fit the bill of my earlier prediction. I concluded, somewhat triumphantly, that my visit to Peru had been pre-ordained. It had enabled me to assist Raul and his family with a possible solution to their problem.

THE CHAUCHILLA NECROPOLIS

As we departed from the amazing Nazca Lines, I realised there was time to spare before the next leg of my journey. It was late morning and both Raul and I were feeling slightly more than peckish. My suggestion that we buy some chicken and chips met with his approval. When we stopped along the road to eat our food, I hesitantly inquired if we might visit the Nazca cemetery. "Sure," said Raul without reserve. He then confirmed that it contained some mummified remains of Nazca people. Also that they had been left exposed for curious eyes to see.

We donated the remnants of our food to a local dog, who had been looking wantonly at us for some time and then we drove off.

The sun was high in the sky as Raul's little car delivered us safely to the necropolis. A large area of desert ground lay before us. The mountains in the distance suggested the presence of gods, who might be watching over the place. A small building housed an office and refreshment facilities. It also afforded the opportunity to purchase an entrance ticket and provided a place to park the car. Inside a partially fenced area of desert ground, stood some waist-high stone-walls. They surrounded sunken square-shaped rooms, about ten feet deep.

Centuries ago, the Nazca people were buried in graves like these, which were designed to resemble the homes they had lived in.

It was a Peruvian archaeologist named Julio C. Tello, who named this style of burial, 'Necropolis.' The corpses were placed seated upright in the foetal position, in the belief that one day they would be reborn. But when that day would be I never found out. The people were buried fully clothed and sometimes their deceased family members would share the same tomb. Placed next to the corpses were some eating and drinking vessels and other everyday items. The graves were exposed many years ago when tomb raiders sacked the area in their quest for buried treasures. Local authorities have brought about some semblance of order to what is left.

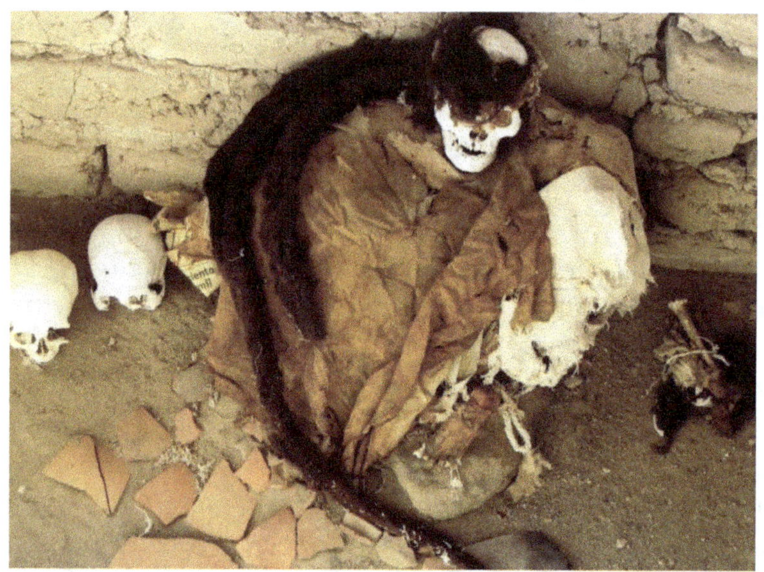

PHOTO NO 9
A MUMMIFIED PERSON HAVING LONG HAIR

There was a well defined pathway which traced a route through the graveyard. It was one that tourists were expected to follow. Raul and I walked along stopping periodically to look inside the open graves. I felt an initial shock when first seeing the 'dead' people but the feeling soon wore off.

I became intrigued by the preservation of the bodies and their clothing. They had remained in a recognisable state, even after many centuries. Here and there, sitting on the smooth surface of a floor, was what looked like a huge pile of clothes needing to be washed. It was in fact the wrapped mummified body of a Nazca person.

Occasionally I saw a brown-coloured foot protruding from the base of such a bundle. Surprisingly, the toe nails were still intact! The heads however, had been reduced to nothing but skulls. But they appeared to have newly grown black hair stemming from them. The skulls were facing upwards and their eyeless sockets appeared to observe any tourists that might happen to pass by.

For a time Raul and I were the only visitors present but a few minutes later a car drove up and two people climbed out. One of them was a young French woman who made her way towards us. The other was a male driver, who happened to be her guide but who chose to wait near the car. Friendly as ever, Raul spoke to the lady. He discovered that her guide, who was a local man, refused to walk into the cemetery due to his superstitious nature. Because of this Raul invited her to join us, with a view to sharing something of the history of the tombs.

We walked together along the path. As Raul was explaining Nazca culture to our 'guest,' I felt a sudden strong compulsion to turn around. As I did so, my eyes fixed upon an open grave. It was one we had walked passed seconds earlier. The two occupants appeared to be looking straight at me. Curiously, it seemed to me that they actually spoke! Not audibly, as one might expect but rather a word sounded inside my head. Clearly, the word, 'Welcome,' was aimed at me. I was taken a little aback. Then a few seconds later I turned to rejoin the others who had carried on ahead. From a distance I saw the young French lady suddenly start to cry.

Perhaps feeling a little embarrassed but most certainly distressed, she bid a speedy farewell and left us to return to her waiting car. I don't know what had caused her to cry but I assumed it was probably the sombre surroundings. She was unaware of my experience, as there had been no time to relate it before she was gone. Perhaps she had also heard a 'voice' speaking to her. Who knows?

Raul told me that he felt uneasy about being in the necropolis and was only making the effort because of my interest. I told him about the little 'message' I had just received and he didn't quite know how to react. Suddenly words came to me that caused me to offer him an explanation. I said, "Do you know something? These people (meaning the deceased) don't faze me. I think they have had a long life and done whatever they were expected to do; when they were living. But now they are 'dead' they are still playing a useful role. By their very presence they are an attraction to thousands of visitors, who arrive each year and learn something about the ancient Nazca culture. Therefore, partly because of them, the history and the memory of the Nazca culture live on." The frown on Raul's face slowly transformed into a smile and he said, "I never thought about it like that before, thank you. I feel much better about being here now."

As we continued our tour I couldn't help noticing small clumps of what looked like sheep's wool, lying on the surface of the desert ground. On closer inspection I also saw scattered around the area, were a variety of fragmented bones. These, I was informed, were the remains of the less fortunate victims of the grave robbers. They had been left unceremoniously there for all to see. I was saddened to witness such a sight and remarked that one doesn't treat a dog with such disrespect. I wished there and then that the Peruvian Government, who has done such a good job to promote tourism and to preserve this site, could give these remains the dignity they deserve.

Raul stated that in recent years, the Peruvian Government had put into force security measures. They were designed to protect the site from further intrusion. He pointed out a small hut that stood in the distance. It looked like an oasis in the middle of a vast desert. In it dwelled a security guard whose job it was to watch over the cemetery after closing time. "But why was the hut so far away from the site?" I asked. Raul explained that the guard preferred to live there because of the nocturnal happenings. It is said that on some nights unearthly noises are heard coming from the area and also strange unexplained lights have been seen hovering nearby.

Perhaps it was our talk about nighttime that prompted me to look at my watch. Instantly I was shocked to see that there was only half an hour remaining before my bus departed from Nazca. With dust clouds billowing from the wheels of Raul's car we made a speedy departure from the site. Later, with little more than a minute to spare, the car rolled to a halt at the Nazca bus station. The engine of the waiting Cruz del Sur bus was ticking over and pushing out diesel fumes, whilst my suit case was loaded on board. With a brief hand shake and the utterance of the words, "Hasta la vista" (until we meet again) the bus and myself along with it, were on our way. As the bus glided along the highway, my mind reflected on the events of the day. It had been exciting from start to finish. I had enjoyed Raul's company and appreciated him taking me to the places we had visited. But what impressed me most was his openness, which I rather think is a Peruvian trait. I sincerely hoped that everything turned out well for him and his family.

****

A VISIT TO PARACAS
****

After travelling for three and a half hours along the main highway towards Lima, the bus finally arrived in the coastal town of Paracas. The guide book stated that it derives its name from the strong winds that often blow along this stretch of the coast. [12]

The time was 1830hrs. Within minutes of being collected from the bus terminus, my eyes were gazing at a beautiful building. A sign near its entrance displayed the name, 'La Hacienda Bahia Paracas'. Try pronouncing those words quickly and with an acquired Spanish accent. Very impressive!

This was to be my place of rest for the night. Considering the grandiose sounding name I expected something special. As it happened I was not to be disappointed. The sight that greeted me was most spectacular. Palm trees festooned the entrance forecourt and discrete lighting illuminated the walk ways. Standing to attention, in front of the plate-glass entrance doors, was a smiling uniformed porter.

"Buenos noches" (Good evening) he said, then promptly offered to relieve me of my suitcase.

As I entered the hotel foyer, my eyes were immediately drawn towards a highly polished desk. It stood at the opposite side of a long and wide reception area. Standing behind it was two bespectacled senoritas. They smiled willingly as they welcomed me to "their" hotel. The formalities began with the usual request for my passport. At every hotel throughout the tour my passport was inspected and it was always photocopied. This was a security measure and probably a way of keeping track of my movements within the country. I usually kept my passport with me, except when there was a mini wall-safe provided in my hotel room.

But even then I was reluctant to use it in case I forgot to retrieve the passport before checking out!

One of the senoritas began to recite a monologue. It was obviously well practised but nonetheless sincere. She listed the hotel's many amenities which included a sauna and surprisingly the use of a catamaran! Apparently the hotel provided some catamarans, which were kept on the nearby beach.

A porter named Carlos, offered to show me to my room. We walked along the splendidly carpeted passageways whilst engaging in small talk. When he became aware that I hailed from Manchester the conversation instantly changed to football. That was a subject about which he was most passionate. In general I found that the average Peruvian male is quite fond of the game.

My bedroom was nothing short of palatial. It accommodated separate twin beds with each having bedside lamps. A bathroom was available en suite with all the usual fittings. They included those little touches of finesse that are seemingly in short supply these days. I mean for example, the tablets of handmade aromatherapy soap. The type containing cottonseed oil and quinoa flakes and together with complementing shampoo. Aside from this there was an unexpected bonus. It was one that caused me to smile. Inside a wardrobe, having transparent glass doors, was a pair of household slippers. They were sealed inside a plastic bag and were obviously for my personal use. But just in case I decided to take them home, across the bridge of the toe-area was printed the hotel's name and logo. Surely this was advertising at its best? Confidentially speaking, I chose not to take the slippers, having decided that the action would be tantamount to theft. But I must confess that the shampoo and the lovely smelling soap accidentally found its way into my suitcase!

Adjacent to the sleeping area was something that caught me by surprise. It was a sunken lounge! Two steps separated the bedroom from what was the lounge. It hosted a settee, with side table and matching reading lamp. Opposite to these was a medium sized card table and two stand chairs. Whilst sited innocuously nearby, was a small but well stocked bar fridge. Predictably there was a flat screen television, having a selection of channels. Two of which had English spoken audio, whilst others had English sub titles and Spanish audio. I found this particularly useful for picking up some essential words of Spanish.

Next morning was June the sixth. Taking a leisurely walk to the restaurant, I passed the large swimming pools that flanked two sides of the hotel. The pools were ideally positioned between the building and a stretch of the Pacific Ocean. They were surrounded by a mixture of sun loungers and palm trees. A grassy area began at the edge of the swimming pools and extended for a short distance towards the beach. The latter comprised of smooth golden sand that stretched in either direction, as far as the eye could see.

The restaurant, in keeping with the general ambience of the hotel, was equally grand. With its seemingly spotless floor, it presented the appearance of a ballroom. Tables and chairs were carefully placed to maximize the available space. At the same time they provided diners with a modicum of privacy. Wall lights illuminated the scene and created soft shadows which offered a relaxed atmosphere. Additionally, a large open fireplace added a homely touch. The placement of a couple of potted trees gave the area a splash of colour and broke up the overall classic look. Placed near the entrance door was a long table that was simply covered with various foodstuffs.

Aside from the usual variety of fresh fruit and various cereals there was a container of newly scrambled eggs. Also there was some freshly baked bread rolls. As a rule Peruvian coffee tasted particularly good and this morning was no exception.

****

After breakfast, at a pre-arranged time, transport arrived to take me to the fishing port of Paracas. A guide escorted me towards a motor launch that was bound for the Ballesta Islands. As we walked along the pathways he pointed to the various species of plant life, which grew nearby. This attention to detail rather impressed me. But what really turned my head was his following suggestion. He said I should go to the toilet before the trip began. He explained that we would be at sea for a couple of hours and there were no on board facilities. I have no doubt that he was considering my age and thought his advice might be necessary. This level of consideration raised my admiration for the guide and my overall confidence in the tour company.

We approached the motor launch which I noticed was fitted with bench seats. They were designed to accommodate twenty-four persons. All was occupied except for one and that was located at the rear of the boat. I soon found myself sitting in it and also next to a couple of senior British citizens. I learned they had travelled from the South of England and were celebrating their wedding anniversary. As it happened, my limited choice of seat proved to be a blessing. Later in the trip it afforded me a good uninterrupted view of the various sights we were fortunate to see.

Before starting out everyone was obliged to don a rather trendy looking life jacket. There was also a brief talk about safety aspects. Suddenly, two large outboard engines, positioned close behind me, burst into life.

They revved up and we were on our way. The roar from the engines was coupled with the forward thrust of the boat. The moderate pounding of the waves against the hull, was followed by the wake our craft created. All of which filled me with an exhilarating feeling.

After a few minutes into our journey the boat slowed down to almost stopping. As it gently rocked from side to side our guide drew our attention to a local landmark. It was known as the 'Tres Cruces' or 'El Candelabro'. A trident shaped figure, looking like three branches of a tree, was sighted on a slope of the northern part of the Paracas peninsula. Allegedly it was created centuries ago by excavating the sand down to the rock base. The colour of the rock contrasted with that of the surrounding surface.

From the top of the outline to the bottom edge is some 130 metres with a width of about 80 metres. [13] Its origin and purpose remain a mystery. One suggestion is that it may have served as a marker for local seamen. The creation was truly an impressive sight. A little time was allowed for the passengers to make photographs before the engines roared into life again and onward we went.

****

A full half hour had passed before our craft reached the Ballestas. The mysterious looking group of rocky islands are situated just north-east of the Paracas peninsula. They are famous for the incredible volume of wildlife that manages to survive there. Strangely though, there are no appreciable quantities of predators, either on the islands or in the skies. Because of this the wildlife is able to prosper and sustain its existence from the food source in the sea. A strong odious odour pervaded the air. No, it wasn't caused by me or any other passenger.

It was the smell of guano, produced by the thousands of birds that choose to make these islands their sanctuary. Many years ago one of the major exports of Peru was guano and much of it came from the Ballesta Islands. At that time people actually lived on the Islands and collected the droppings to be exported for use as a very effective fertilizer. In this present age, the valuable product is only collected every four years.

As my sense of smell was adjusting itself to the putrid stench, my ears were bombarded by the tumultuous sounds of the feathered residents. Many sizes and species of birds were to be seen. They were either flying about or nestling on the steep cliffs. It truly was a bird watcher's paradise. Our very informative guide pointed out the various species of birds to the less knowledgeable amongst our group. I may have been the least knowledgeable of all but the experience was nonetheless enlightening and enjoyable. Some of the names I managed to remember were the blackish oyster catcher, the guanay, (a bird that had a white patch near its eye), Peruvian boobies and the red legged cormorant. I understand the latter is on the endangered species list. Also, I think I heard the guide say there was only fifteen of them alive. Can that be possible?

Another bird I remember seeing is the Inca tern, with their red beak and matching legs. Besides the birds there were also large groups of Humboldt penguins. But most surprisingly there was two large sea-lions. They made barking sounds whilst clinging to the rocks as best they could. The breeding season for sea-lions is mostly between the months of November and February and after which they move on. So it would seem that this pair had simply been left behind.

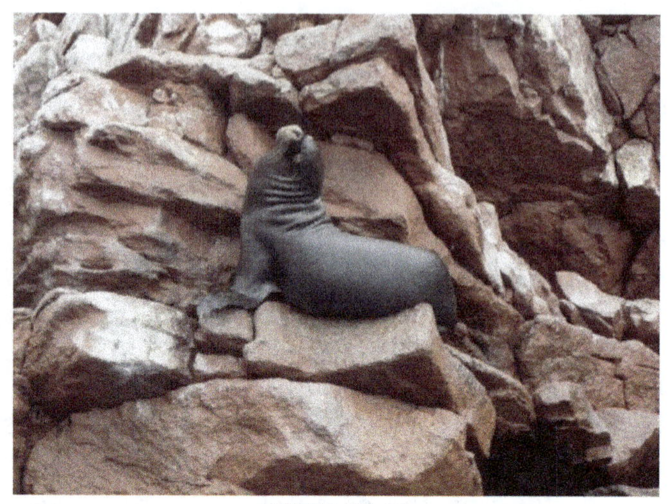

At various places amongst the rocks, was the abandoned equipment of the 19th century installations. They had been used for guano extraction. At a section of a nearby cliff face I noticed a narrow seam that was black in colour and ran throughout its length. Our guide was quick to inform me that it was basalt. We motored to where the seam petered out and then our boat passed through an open ended cave. It had been formed by sea-wave erosion and it allowed us access to the other face of the outcrop.

By looking at the many rock formations, which are a spectacle in themselves, the erosive nature of the sea can best be appreciated. At one place two large holes had been eroded through the rock and were allowing the sea water to pass through them. The holes were evenly spaced apart and positioned at sea level. They presented to the viewer the impression that they might be a pair of eye sockets, placed into some giant skull that appeared to be rising up from the briny!

The visit to these islands had lasted for the best part of an hour and now it was time to return to the mainland.

Once more the outboard engines burst into life and propelled us at a fast pace in the direction of the Paracas shoreline. During the homeward trip I casually glanced to the starboard side of the craft. I caught sight of a singular bird in the far distance. It was flying at a level just three or four feet above the surface of the sea. I couldn't help admiring the stamina of the winged animal. The bird was able to keep up with us for a considerable time before finally turning away to head for the opposite shoreline. It seemed to me as though our feathered friend was escorting us from its none-human world, before finally bidding us farewell.

FLIGHT OF THE PSEUDO BIRD

Once safely returned to the hotel there was a couple of hours to 'kill' before I was due to leave Paracas and head back to Lima. I decided to take a leisurely walk along the beach that was noticeably unpopulated by human form. Before long my eyes focused on a makeshift wooden pier that loomed in the distance. From the smooth sandy beach it poked out into the sea. It unwittingly provided a resting perch for a number of cormorants, which squawked noisily at the sky. As I walked at a steady pace, I saw various species of birds frolicking in the sea and passing the time of day. One of which was a large pelican. It clumsily ducked and dived, as it caught fish with its inimitable beak. Soon after, it greedily swallowed them.

Drawing closer to the pier I noticed another winged wonder. It had the appearance of a bird of prey. Patiently I watched as it 'hung' almost motionless in the sky. It seemingly used thermal air currents to keep it aloft. Towering above the perched cormorants for over a half hour it presented a formidable sight.

With my limited knowledge of winged predators I surmised this one to be a frigate bird. The frigate bird is said to have the largest wingspan, in comparison to its body, of any species in the world. On occasions, they have been known to stay in the air for the best part of a week. Half an hour was hardly a week but it certainly seemed a long time for any bird to stay airborne. Especially since it flew neither upwards nor downwards, but simply remained static!

I must confess it was quite some time before I eventually noticed a taught wire, which was attached to the bird's beak. On closer visual inspection the whole picture became clearer. I saw that the wire had originated from a fishing rod that was strapped to an upright post, which in turn belonged to the pier. To all intents and purposes the 'bird' was flying in the same manner as a kite!

The purpose of this 'flying bird' finally dawned on me. It was actually placed there to deter the cormorants from catching fish and thus prevent them from spoiling the sport of would-be fishermen!

What an idiot I had been. But in all fairness, the 'bird' looked authentic and certainly fooled me. But had it fooled the cormorants? Well, safe to say that during the time I observed this pseudo 'bird,' none of the cormorants moved from their perched positions. Perhaps it had indeed, fooled them too!

The time spent on that priceless beach had been wonderful. The experience had allowed me to observe a capsule of nature in the raw. Sadly it was time for me to return to the hotel and once again, to pack my suitcase. I say 'pack my suit case' but the truth is that it was never fully unpacked for the duration of my holiday!

I placed it in the hotel's reception area under the watchful eyes of the senoritas. Then I spent a few minutes by sending some e-mails from the hotel's courtesy computer. One of the nice features of this tour was that at every hotel, of which I visited, there was an internet connection. It enabled me to keep in touch with overseas family and friends.

At the allotted time a locally appointed guide arrived to take me to the bus station. In the hotel foyer a tall man walked towards me. 'Mucho gusto' (Pleased to meet you) I said, practising a little more of the Spanish I had mastered. A smile erupted on the guide's face as he responded in English by saying, "Pleased to meet you too."

At precisely 15:15hrs after allowing for a brief delay, the bus bound for Lima set off. Its departure was celebrated by a glorious sun-set.

It was late in the evening when the bus arrived at Lima but Viator's on-the-ball efficiency was working overtime. A taxi was waiting to ferry me to the Hotel El Tambo, and that was where I was to spend a second night.

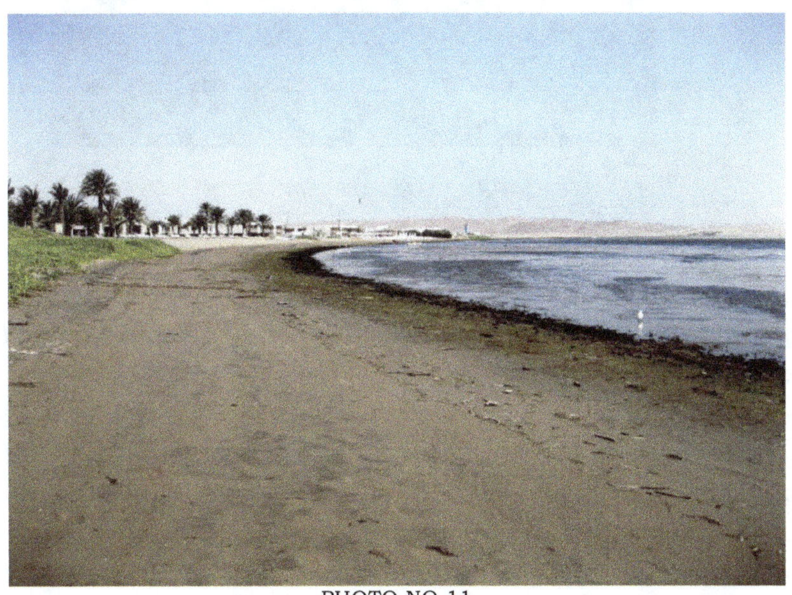

PHOTO NO 11
PARACAS BEACH WITH MY HOTEL IN THE DISTANCE

FROM LIMA TO CUSCO

****

On June the seventh I travelled to the City of Cusco, the ancient capital of the Inca Empire. My starting point was Lima airport. It was a pleasant place being both modern and compact. It had the usual amenities that a traveller expects but best of all was the departure gate. From there I intended to board a jet plane that was bound for Cusco. Hanging prominently from the roof space was a large and easy to read sign.

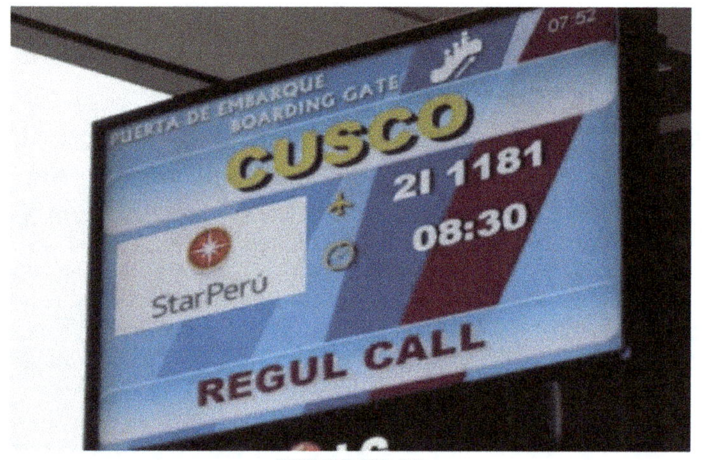

PHOTO NO 12
THE SIGN AT THE BOARDING GATE

Its colourful letters displayed the destination, flight number and present time of day. They helped to make my waiting period more tolerable and reassured me to know I was at the right place.
The flight lasted a little over an hour. But the time passed quickly, when I started up a conversation with a lady passenger. It transpired that she worked for a golfing channel with an American TV station. It was based in sunny California. Meeting interesting people is just one of the many perks of distance travel. But just as the conversation was starting to fascinate me, a steward

interjected and handed out some complimentary refreshments. Whilst biting into a freshly made, cheese-filled bread roll, my attention was drawn to the view from the port-side window. The distant snow covered Andes mountain range, looked magnificent beneath a pale blue sky.

After landing at Cusco's miniscule airport, I waited patiently at the baggage collection point for the arrival of my suitcase. Apparently, as I was watching for the case, someone nearby was watching me! It turned out that the 'stalker' was one of the locals who made a small income by carrying visitors' bags. The mature looking man must have been hard of hearing. He ignored my exclamation of "That's OK I'll carry the bag myself!" "After all", I thought, "That's why there are little wheels attached to its base!" But as we approached the waiting courtesy bus, with its crew standing alongside, the obliging helper winked at a guide. He triumphantly announced, "Hah, I've got my tip for today!"

Having fulfilled the obligatory formalities, of showing my travel voucher and passport, to yet another willing tour guide; the courtesy bus was on its way. Cusco is a fascinating location with a fuse of old and relatively new buildings. Many of the newer structures have been built on or over the ruins of earlier Inca architecture. During my visit I was destined to see a number of the latter. Within a few minutes the bus arrived at the hotel where I was to spend the next three days.

On reflection it appeared to have two names, although I never thought to ask why. The first name was 'Palacio Imperial Cusco.' Without wishing to win any prize, I should think that if the name was translated into English, it would read 'Imperial Palace'. However, after entering the hotel and checking its amenities, I thought that the title might be stretching one's imagination.

The second title was perhaps more to the point as it read, 'Mabey Hotel'. "Yes", I thought, "I could go along with that one. 'Maybe' (sic) it could be a hotel". I reminded myself as to what the brochure had to say about it:

> *'The hotel is located in the middle of the forest, mountains and representative population of the Valle Sangrado, (Sacred Valley) in a perfect environment to relax and feel the magic of the Andes.'*

In all fairness, the mountains were visible, albeit at some distance from the hotel. As for the forest; I think that the trees must have been cut down long ago because the present building was surrounded by various properties.

At the hotel reception a kindly member of staff informed me that my room was not quite ready. I was invited to take a seat. and then asked "Would you like a cup of tea while you wait?" Considering I was going nowhere at that moment I accepted the offer.

The tea arrived and was placed on to a table next to me. "How odd" I thought. I had never seen tea like that before. Large tea leaves, each about the size of my big-toe nail, floated on the surface of steaming, green coloured water. The concoction looked every bit like an Irish stew that had gone terribly wrong!

I learned that the leaves were from the coca plant and that the 'tea' was good for alleviating the effects of altitude sickness. This seemed to be fortuitous as Cusco is located at some 11000 feet above sea-level and the air has a lower oxygen content. The effect upon a person breathing the rarefied air is to become de-hydrated. This can cause severe headaches and sometimes even vomiting.

Feeling my head tightening, as though a slow moving vice was being applied to my forehead, I wasted no time in swallowing the 'witches brew'. Coca, so I was informed, grows in the valleys and upper jungle regions of the Andean range and the leaves are used to produce the drug, cocaine. Sometimes the locals chew a leaf or two, which produce a pleasant numbness in the mouth and leave a pungent but pleasant taste. The effect of chewing the leaves produces a mild stimulant and helps to suppress the feelings of hunger, thirst, and even pain. Frankly, I suspect the cocaine might have a bearing on that!

The sign above the entrance to the Mabey Hotel sported a three star rating. When I eventually saw my room I was tempted to say, "Yeah, you can see the three stars through a hole in the ceiling!" But perhaps I was being a little harsh. Considering that 50 U.S. Dollars was the daily charge for bed and breakfast, one shouldn't expect too much. At least the bed linen appeared to be clean and the bathroom was fully stocked with soap and towels. It's just that the room smelt musty, which I think was due to there being no direct daylight.

By way of contrast I must say the hotel staff was very courteous and it did have a computer together with WiFi for public use. There was also an occasion during my stay when I employed the hotel's laundry service. A small request-form was available, which I duly completed. It arranged for the cleaning of one pair of underpants, one pair of socks and two shirts. The total cost was 10 U.S. Dollars! "Not bad at all" I thought.

My room was located on the second floor and although a staircase afforded access, a small elevator was my chosen mode of travel. Banging sounds produced by workmen, as they carried out hotel internal repairs, heralded my arrival to the room. Together with my increasing headache, the noise induced me to deposit the case and make a bee line for the exit. I decided to make the most of the day by venturing forth into the unknown. Well, at least to have a walk along the nearby streets!

At the lower end of Avenue El Sol was a grassy area called the 'Parque Orellana Pumaqchupan.' A vacant bench provided a place to enjoy the warming rays of the sun. But the nearby street traffic was thick and noisy, with horns sounding a plenty. Thus I was prevented from having any form of sleep. As I watched the populace passing by, I noticed that they appeared to have a lower standard of living, compared to those of Lima.

A man walked along carrying a large black bin-liner. He was collecting empty plastic bottles, which I presume he would exchange for a few Soles. Seconds later a small framed, sun-tanned man and having a smiling face, approached me. With an outstretched hand he offered a paper tract. I glanced down and read the title words: 'El Ocultismo'. (The Occult) Accepting his little gift I looked up and into his eyes. They seemed to be smiling as he pointed towards the sky. Not a word was spoken between us but his simple gesture and the two printed Spanish words said it all!

Sat on the grass opposite from me was a young couple. They were engaged in deep conversation. Within a few minutes a policeman arrived and walked determinedly towards them. He was wearing a flat peaked hat and a dark blue uniform. A white leather Sam Browne completed the image. The two parties exchanged a few calm words, after which the couple moved away. As they did so the policeman walked off triumphantly, in the opposite direction.

It was plain to see that loitering, or at any rate, sitting on the grass was against the law. The policeman wore a uniform that I believe was unique to his job. Which appeared to be that of monitoring the park areas.

During my stay in Peru I saw a variety of uniforms as worn by employees of the Police Department. I suspect they each represented a different level of responsibility.

To my mind this seemed like a good idea, considering that a uniformed person could be trained to fulfil a specific job description. But at the same time, that person could have the authority to deal with other situations, should they present themselves. Perhaps a salary was paid accordingly. If so, the cost to the state would be minimised but the number of people employed would be maximised. As I saw it, besides providing a vital service to the community, the Peruvian Government was creating much needed jobs for its people.

At length an elderly lady ambled along a tarred path, in front of where I was sitting. She wore a brown trilby hat, of a type that was common amongst many of the locals. Her brown chunky jersey looked out of place against her brightly coloured dress. It was made from cotton and printed with a blue and white floral design. Carrying a large plastic bag, she walked along with the help of a walking stick. It had a curious kink in it; about the midpoint of its length. Perhaps what singled her out from the average passerby, were her spindly legs. Covering them was a pair of knitted stockings. One of which was fully pulled up and sported a couple of large holes. The other was rolled completely down. A pair of seemingly oversized boots that ended just above her ankles, completed her attire. As she waddled along at a moderate pace, the sight of her boots commanded my attention. I was instantly reminded of Walt Disney's Minnie the mouse!

My eyes followed the lady as she continued until reaching the end of the path. Perhaps resulting from an acquired habit, she stopped alongside a litter bin. Leaning forward she quickly caught a glimpse of the inside. Her trained eyes must have seen that there was nothing worth taking. Appearing to be unperturbed, she moved off gracefully into the distance!

I was beginning to enjoy my little siesta in the warming sunshine. Once again my thoughts were disturbed by the arrival of another candidate who was vying for my observation. A woman, who at a guess was in her mid-twenties and looking European in her features, approached a nearby bench. Her slender form was dressed in denim trousers that were flared at the ankles. They put me in mind of a style I had not seen since the 1970's. But then fashions come and go as we all know. Her hair looked singularly unkempt as it was formed into long ringlets. They hung like strings of sausages, in a butcher's shop window. A pair of thick-rimmed sun-glasses disguised her eyes. Over a shoulder hung a thin canvas bag. She proceeded to open it whilst stooping to sit on the bench. From the bag she pulled out the bits and pieces necessary for rolling a marijuana 'joint'. A few seconds later she lit her creation and puffed away. Once the desired effect had been achieved, the young lady drew her legs up towards her body. Her knees were touching her chin as she dozed off into a blissful sleep. I mused to myself, at least this time there was no policeman to move her along. The thought faded but gave way to another. It was time for me to return to the hotel. Transport was expected to arrive and would take me on a tour of Cusco City.

****

Built at an altitude of 11,200 feet and surrounded by even higher mountains, Cusco has a wealth of churches and plazas, along with fountains and remnants of Inca architecture. It has been continuously occupied for at least 2000 years and claims to be the oldest city in the Americas. Modern day Peru has been shaped by its Inca heritage and the relatively recent Spanish invasion.

Religion was imperative to both cultures, and its presence can still be felt today. Before the Spanish invaded Peru the Inca religion was characterized by their physical environment. Surrounded by unpredictable and dangerous landscapes, the Incas were at the mercy of the elements. They believed that natural forces were actually deities, and in order to protect themselves against the dangers of nature, they had to venerate and honour the world around them. Adhering to the idea of duality, the Incas believed that each force had an opposing force. Homeostasis could only be maintained between humans and nature through a reciprocal exchange of worship and use of the land.

The religion of the Inca Empire emphasized a pantheon of six gods. Viracocha, Inti, Illapa, Pachamama, Mamaquilla, and Cochamama are the names of gods who presided over creation, the sun, the weather, the Earth, the moon and the oceans respectively. Religion was a constant force in daily life, and even the emperor was considered semi-divine.

One Inca myth told of a time when the humans were wild. Inti looked down on the people and felt sorry for them, so he sent two of his children, a boy and a girl, to teach the people how to live. He gave his children a golden rod and instructed them to jab it into the ground wherever they went. Where the rod sank into the ground without resistance, he declared that is where they should start their civilization. That place, according to myth, was Cusco. The children began the Inca civilization, and all the successive rulers are descendants of them and thus, descendants of Inti. The name Inca actually translates to mean 'children of the sun'.

****

CUSCO CITY SIGHTS

A small coach arrived at the hotel to ferry me to the hills high above the City. On this latest tour I was one of a party of five. As it happened all were English speaking. Our tour guide was a delightful man. When asked his name, he replied "Well, my friends call me Chico." From then on his name was 'Chico' and we were all his friends. Cusco was the capital of the Inca Empire but today it survives only in its ruins imbued with an atmosphere of mystery and grandeur.

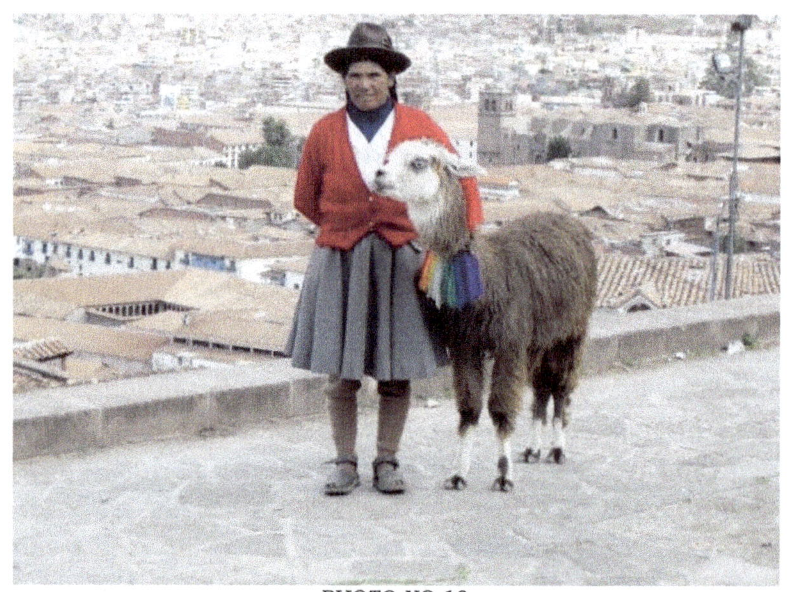
PHOTO NO 13
A PERUVIAN FARMER WITH A FRIEND

The Spanish colonial city, with its attractive pink tiled roofs, arcaded plazas and steep winding alleyways, stands upon previously used Inca foundation stones. Amongst the terra cotta roof-tops are the principal buildings of the city. In the centre is the Plaza De Armas on which stands the Cathedral of Santo Domingo. It has been suggested that when the Incas constructed the various streets, their layout was completed in the shape of a giant puma. To the Inca the puma represented both strength and the middle world in which they lived.

Our coach stopped at an open-spaced parapet that afforded a commanding view over the sprawling city. In attendance were some ladies who were dressed in traditional costume. They were dutifully aided by some docile looking llamas.

The day was bright and cheery. The mountains in the distance and the brooding clouds gathering in the sky, presented a spectacular sight.

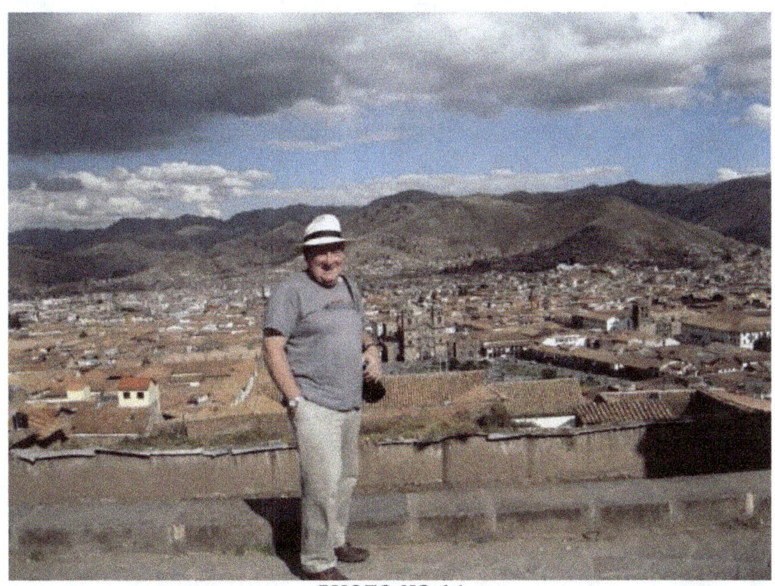
PHOTO NO 14
THE AUTHOR WITH THE CITY OF CUSCO IN THE DISTANCE

A cluster of tourists along with our little group, gathered around the posing ladies and their faithful llamas. Photographs were made and afterwards some coinage was offered. The posers were thanked for being there. Chico politely announced that when we were ready, he would take us to see the local San Pedro Market Hall. It was there that all manner of food items could be bought.

THE SAN PEDRO MARKET HALL

The San Pedro Market Hall is an old steel-framed building. Its coating of red oxide paint has faded and is stained with droppings from numerous pigeons. They perch on its corrugated tin roof and watch with suspicious eyes, everyone who passes through its doors. The words 'Bienvenidos a tu Mercado San Pedro' are displayed on a brightly coloured sign. It contrasts noticeably with the building to which it is attached.

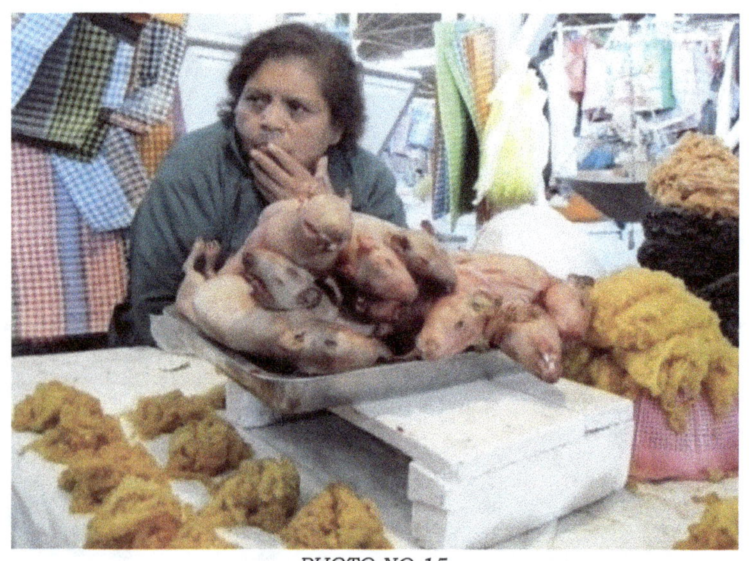

PHOTO NO 15
A PERUVIAN STALL HOLDER SELLING READY TO COOK GUINEA PIGS

The floor of the hall is paved with stone slabs and plays host to scores of stalls that display a multitude of goods. Cuy, or guinea pigs (dead ones) were for sale, along with a variety of indigenous food stuffs. One thing I instantly recognised was coca leaves. They had been the main ingredient of the 'witches brew' I drank at the Mabey Hotel. I simply couldn't leave without buying a few packets. Another stall had portions of cut meat for sale. It was placed alongside the carcass of a pig that hung from a nearby support pillar.

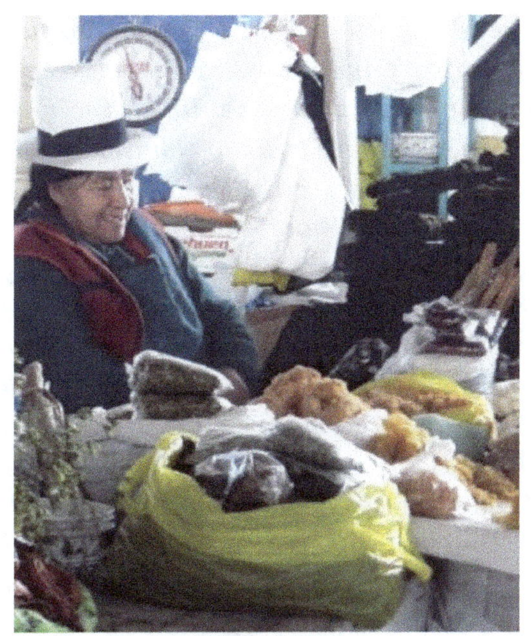

PHOTO NO 16
A LADY WITH WHITE HAT AND BLACK BAND

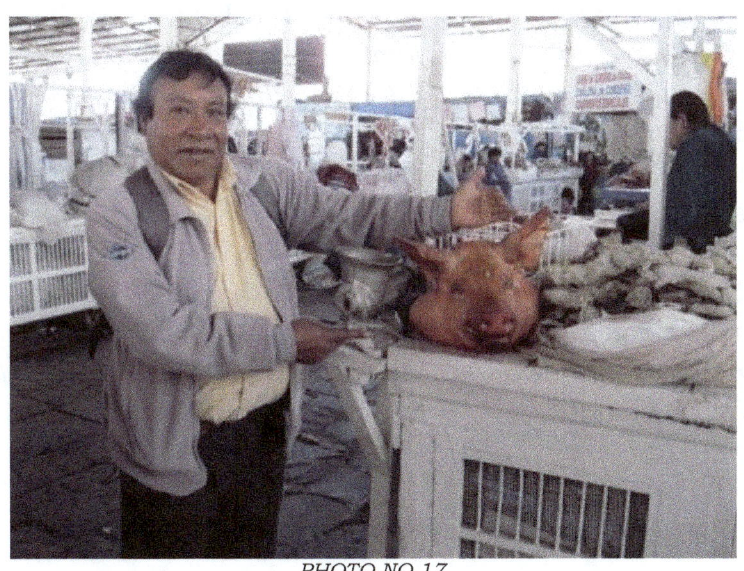

PHOTO NO 17
PICTURED LEFT IS CHICO WHO WAS OUR FRIEND AND GUIDE

Next to that was something I presumed had previously belonged to the carcass. It was the smiling head of a pig! By way of contrast there was a stall that was covered with a variety of fruit and vegetables; the like of which I had never seen before. Being cautious I decided to sample a couple of bananas. They were something with which I was familiar. What a magnificent taste they had! The people selling their wares presented a fascinating spectacle. In particular were the senior women who sat at their stalls. Their eyes watched a person's every move and their faces reflected a lifetime of experience. Most were blasé to the fact that they were being photographed. Some smiled at me and one even shook my hand! Some of the lady stall holders wore white straw hats that sported a broad black-band around the brim. The hats proudly but silently testified that the ladies were descendants of the Inca and that Inca blood flowed in their veins.

Meanwhile people bustled through the passages to get at the wares. Surprisingly some of the locals had brought their children along. They in turn, had brought their toys and were allowed to play with them in the aisles. It wasn't unusual to see a child scurrying along on the back of a small four-wheeled quad bike! The scene presented one of a relaxed family atmosphere that was most enjoyable to watch. The market adventure drew to a close and Chico conducted our little group back to the waiting coach. We gravitated towards the city centre and arrived at our next port of call. It was the Cathedral of Santo Domingo.

VISIT TO CUSCO CATHEDRAL

The Plaza de Armas is the name of Cusco's central square. On it stands the Cathedral of Santo Domingo. Begun in 1550, it was completed a hundred years later. Stones were taken from the deserted Inca fortress of Sacsayhuaman to supply the construction. It was built in the Baroque style, on the foundations of the earlier Inca palace of Virachocha, who was the Inca creator god. Inside the Cathedral are sights and treasures that simply blow one's mind. One of them is a huge altar that is made from solid gold and studded with precious stones. Its central part is covered in pure silver. The gold and silver were re-cycled from captured Inca treasures, at the time of the Spanish invaders, or 'Conquistadores' as they are often called.

Apart from this spectacle, there are some fascinating examples of oil paintings to be seen. One of which was painted by Marcos Zapata, which depicts the famous Biblical Last Supper. However, his particular version has created a Latin American style. It has for the main dish, which sits in the centre of the table, a cuy, or guinea pig! Also standing on the table, are bottles of chicha, which is an alcoholic brew, made from fermented maize.

The figure of Judas can be seen at the front left of the painting. He is holding a leather bag that presumably contains the infamous thirty pieces of silver. The viewer's attention is drawn to his face. It is painted in a darker hue to that of the other disciples. Rather eerily, his eyes seem to follow the spectator when walking to the left or to the right of the painting. Another painting, which is displayed near to the main entrance of the building, portrays an image of Santa Maria. It too has eyes that seem to follow the viewer!

****

THE KORICANCHA TEMPLE

The Koricancha Temple, or Sun Temple, as it is also known was the Inca Empire's most important edifice and was dedicated to Inti, the Inca sun god. According to legend, the site of the Sun Temple is where Inti's golden rod sank into the ground.

The reader may remember that Inti sent his two children to earth with a golden rod. They were instructed to push the rod into the ground and where it sank without resistance was where they should start a civilisation.

Some of the Inca's greatest artwork was housed in the Sun Temple, being the epicentre of the Inca's spiritual life. The walls of the temple were covered in gold leaf, with ornate designs and depictions etched in it. After the Spanish conquest, the Spaniards removed the gold, destroyed the temple and built a church on top of its foundations. Today the church is called The Convent of Santo Domingo and portions of the original Inca Temple are visible beneath its walls. It is symbolic of both the fall of the Inca Empire and the subsequent Catholic dominance.

The visit to the Convent of Santo Domingo marked the end of the day's tour for our group of five. We bade a sad farewell to Chico, our friendly guide and we were returned to our respective hotels.

RUINS OF SACSAYHUAMAN

Next morning was June the eighth. As I enjoyed a leisurely hotel breakfast, the sun made an appearance above some distant mountains. A few minutes later a mini-bus arrived to take me to see some of the historical sites of Cusco. I felt privileged since I was the only passenger aboard the bus. However, the feeling dissolved as it arrived at another hotel. Four tourists climbed onboard and surprisingly they all spoke English.

One lady was actually from Manchester (U.K.) and two others had travelled from the neighbouring country of Chile. The fourth person was a U.K. man in his early fifties. We later discovered he was employed as a fire-fighter in the City of London.

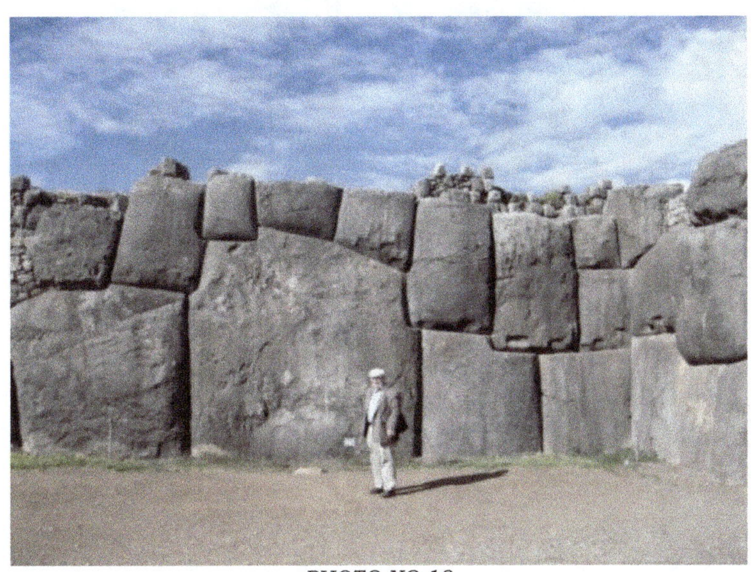

PHOTO NO 18
THE AUTHOR AT SACSAYHUAMAN

After a short but brisk journey the bus stopped on a hillside overlooking the sprawl of Cusco. We had arrived at a place called Sacsayhuaman. Our futile attempts at pronouncing the name caused us some merriment and a little concern. But all was appeased by our wily guide who advised us to call the place 'sexy woman.'
The site had been developed over a period of seventy-seven years and towards the end of the 1400's became an important Inca stronghold. Surrounding the site are gigantic fortress walls. They consist of almost megalith stones which were placed together without any need for mortar. The precision with which they fit is truly impressive when one considers that the largest stone is estimated to weigh some seventy tons!

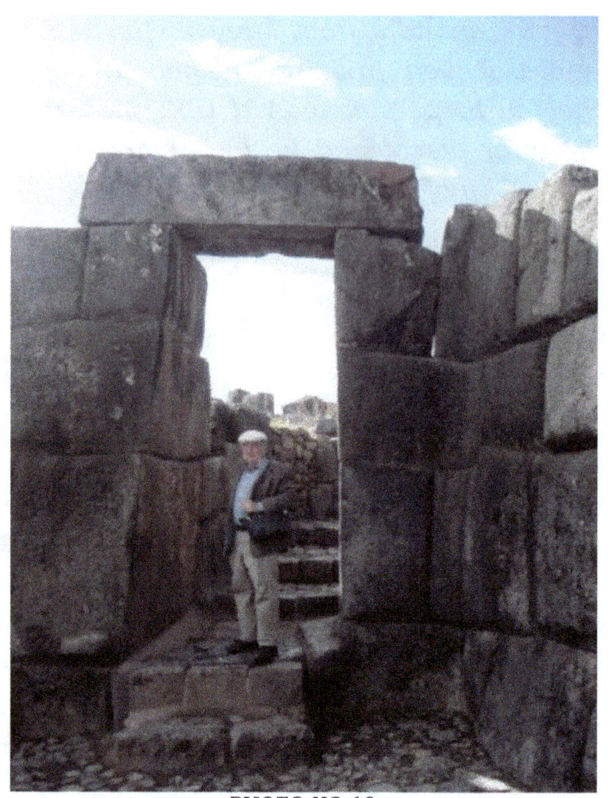

PHOTO NO 19
THE AUTHOR STANDING IN AN INCA DOORWAY

The ruins are truly spectacular and not only for their precision of construction but also for the monumental size of each block. Standing amidst this scene of splendour, it is hard to imagine that on the site, in the year 1536, an epic battle took place. The Spanish conquerors and the Inca warriors fought a bloody contest during which hundreds of lives were lost.

The Conquistadores were victorious and later set about destroying the fortress. All that remains today represents only approximately twenty per cent of the original.

As the day progressed our little band of curious visitors became friends. Together we wandered about the stones whilst gazing in awe at their enormity.

Considering that some were almost the size of a London bus we were dumbstruck to explain how they got there. At one time during our walk, we were taken completely by surprise when a llama happened to cross our path. The fire-fighter reached out in the hope he might stroke the animal. He asked our guide, "Is it true that they spit at you when they get angry?" As the guide was answering "Si" (Yes), the llama made a hasty retreat. Without proving the action one way or another, it quickly disappeared amongst the rocks!

THE TEMPLE OF Q'ENQO

Another site our group surveyed was called Q'enqo or Qenko and is known as the Temple of the Puma god. It initially appeared to be nothing more than some large rocks and a couple of small rooms. But on closer inspection it became apparent that the site has a semi-circular amphitheatre. Additionally, there are underground galleries that were used for ceremonial purposes. It also has its own altar, which according to our trusted guide, is where it is believed that human sacrifices once took place. Not wishing to run the risk of history repeating itself, we hot-footed it back to the coach park.

Although feeling safer away from the Temple, it was at the coach park that we encountered another kind of threat. This came in the form of a local lady, who wished to sell us a souvenir! From her limited selection of items; I bought what I thought was something rather special. It was a small replica of an Inca cross and made from flat polished stone. The arms of the cross were of equal length and represented the four corners of the Inca Empire. In the centre was a small hole which signified that Cusco had been the Empire's central point.

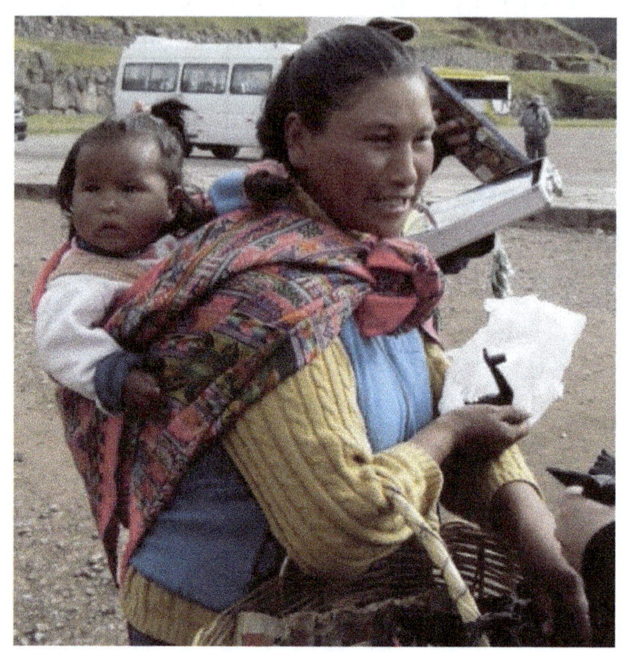

PHOTO NO 20
A PERUVIAN LADY SELLING SOUVENIRS

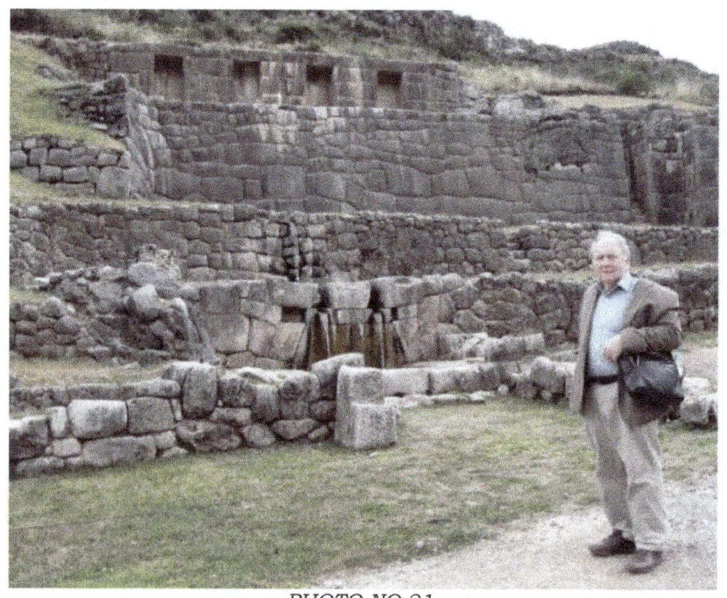

PHOTO NO 21
THE AUTHOR AT TAMBOMACHAY

Situated not far from the coach park was another place of interest and it was called Tambomachay. It consisted of a series of aqueducts, canals and waterfalls that run through the terraced rocks. Located some eleven kilometres from Cusco and placed at an approximate height of 3765 metres above sea level, the function of the site remains a mystery. It has been suggested that they may have served as a spa resort for the Inca political elite. Alternatively it might have been a military outpost for guarding the approach to Cusco. One guide book even makes the suggestion that it was a temple used for the worship of the water god. The book also points out that the flow of water from the canals is the same throughout the year.

Before leaving the ruins and heading back to the centre of Cusco, some time was spared to observe two farmers. They were digging in a nearby field.

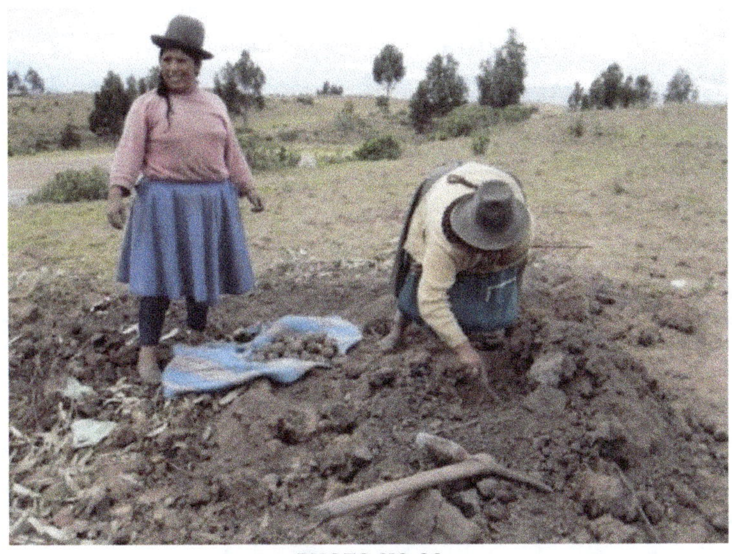

PHOTO NO 22
PERUVIAN FARMERS DIG FOR BAKED POTATOES

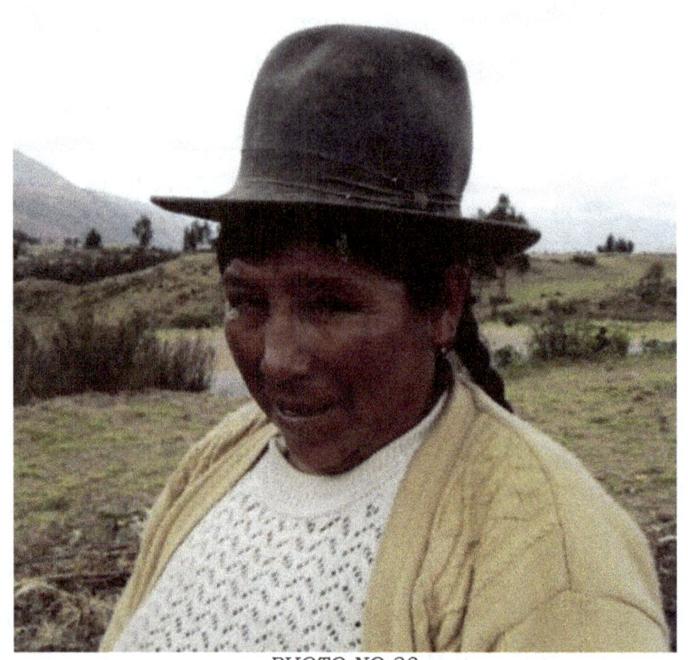
PHOTO NO 23
A PERUVIAN FARMER POSES

Prior to our arrival they had baked some potatoes in the traditional manner. They had placed them beneath the hot embers from a wood burning fire. Noting our interest the farmers offered to let us sample their wares. The hot jacketed potato dug from the heated Peruvian earth, tasted delicious. Perhaps by being at a height of over three and a half thousand metres simply added to the experience.

Whilst consuming the hot baked spud, I happened to see a lady who was working in an adjacent field. She was actually hand-spinning wool and furthermore, judging by her onlookers she appeared to have no shortage of raw material! [See Photo No 24]

The day's tour was coming to an end and our little group had bonded nicely. So much so that it was suggested we should find a restaurant and enjoy a meal together.

The Chilean ladies, who had visited Cusco in the past, knew of a suitable restaurant. It offered a commanding view overlooking the town square. The square of course was where the annual festivities of Corpus Christi were to take place. The choice of restaurant seemed to be ideal. But as it happened, the bus dropped us off some distance from it and we were obliged to walk.

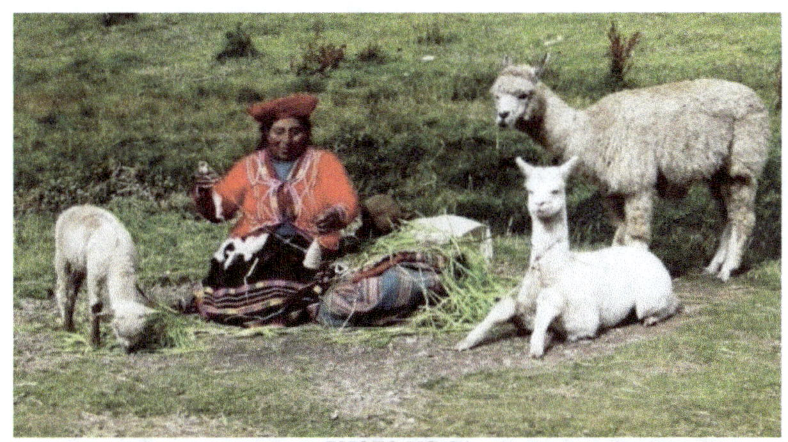

PHOTO NO 24
PERUVIAN LADY SPINNING WOOL WITH HER ONLOOKERS

Little did we know that awaiting us in a nearby street was a pleasant surprise. We encountered a large gathering of people and a multi-piece band. They stood together with one of the many festival biers that were to be seen later that day. As if by some special arrangement upon seeing our approach, the band struck up! With a resounding crash of a giant pair of cymbals and the beat of a big bass drum, the procession began. Like mechanical toys that had just been wound up its members moved slowly along the street. Some carried the bier that supported an effigy of their chosen saint. Their destination was the city square.
Clarinets took the dominant lead in the host of musical instruments.

Collectively they produced a mix of sounds that resonated in my ears. The clash of cymbals punctuated the melody and the bass drum kept everyone on track. I got busy with my camcorder and soon became carried away with the spectacle of it all. Eventually I found myself not only walking with the procession but actually shoulder to shoulder with the band members!

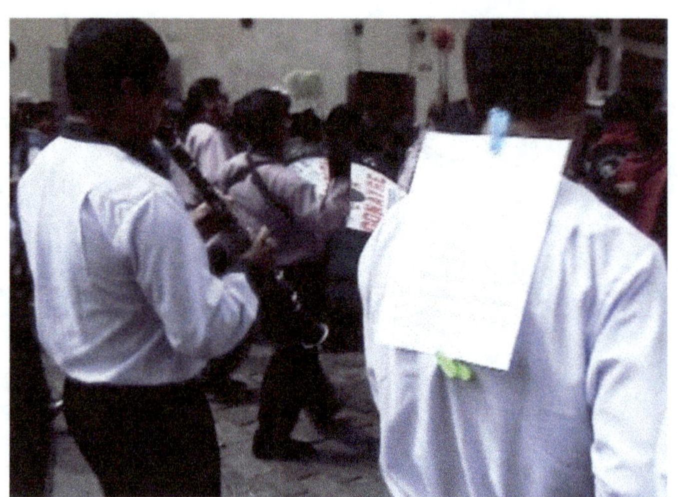

PHOTO NO 25
MUSICIANS ON THE MARCH WITH PEGGED MUSIC

No one batted an eyelid or murmured a word of complaint because of my presence and once again I felt privileged to be accepted.
What I couldn't help noticing was that various members of the band had a unique way of reading music. They had attached a sheet of the music to the back of a friend's shirt. The ingenious method by which this was achieved was to use, of all things; plastic clothes pegs!
[See Photo No 25]

CORPUS CHRISTI

Every year during the month of June and some sixty days following Easter Sunday, there is a festival at Cusco called Corpus Christi. It is a celebration of both Christian and pagan beliefs. For the Christian believers Corpus Christi is celebrated by carrying effigies of ten different saints and five virgins in various processions. For days before the event craftsmen make sure the effigies are cleaned and restored to perfection. The processions proceed from different parts of Cusco and culminate in a grand gathering in the city square of Plaza de Armas.

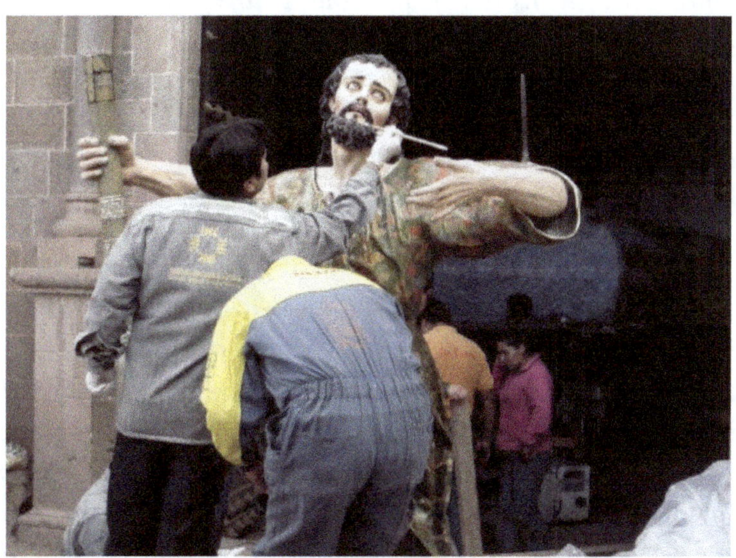

PHOTO NO 26
PUTTING FINISHING TOUCHES TO ONE OF THE EFFIGIES

The people chosen to carry the various effigies wear respectful clothing and ensure that their exhibit appears at its best on this special day. A multitude of the general public gathers to enjoy the spectacle which is enhanced by music produced by the many musicians.

People of all ages, children, parents and grandparents, gather to celebrate the event. There is an invigorating and contagious atmosphere present during this colourful spectacle. The different effigies are carried lovingly, although not without much effort. They are each mounted on an individual wooden bier. Each is carried by a number of specially chosen strong, young men.

I watched one such team comprised of thirty men, with their faces grimaced, as they moved slowly passed me. They made their way towards the Cathedral. The chosen men must have experienced much discomfort as the bier rested on their shoulders. Ultimately each effigy is taken into the confines of the Cathedral. There it is safely deposited and is blessed by the clergy. Walking in line behind and in front of the biers are dignitaries, local councillors and townspeople. They all come to share this annual experience. All the while an army of street cleaners, wearing their distinctive two piece blue overalls and matching baseball caps, are busy at work. Whilst wielding sweeping brushes and shovels, they manually keep the square and adjacent streets clear from litter.

****

The celebrations officially began from about 1100hrs. This was more or less the time our little group had found the restaurant and were enjoying a tasty meal. From a lofty dining room we saw the annual spectacle unfolding in the square beneath us. Slowly but surely it filled with a colourful assembly of people. Soon after the meal was finished, my friends announced that they had to return to their hotel. Although they invited me along, I was so captivated by the evolving events that I chose to stay behind. We did arrange to meet later in the afternoon but sadly I never saw them again.

Essentially there were three main sources of activity in the square that day. One was the slow, noisy and constant arrival of the various wooden biers. Amongst a throng of spectators was a succession of effigies of revered saints. They could be seen to bob up and down and to sway from side to side, on their way to the Cathedral. The motion was caused by the teams of selected men, who bore the weight of the biers on their shoulders. They weaved a course through the dense gathering of people.

Another source of activity was provided by a number of male participants, who were dressed as farmers of the field. They wore dark leggings and a colourful woollen shawl. Meanwhile their identity was preserved by the donning of a knitted, balaclava-type head piece, which was white in colour. Whilst gathered in front of the Cathedral they proceeded to act out a pseudo religious ritual. Initially each farmer arrived carrying a lamb draped across his shoulders. Thankfully, the lambs were hand-made woollen facsimiles. They placed them with care onto the ground.

Aiding the farmers was a local band of musicians, who played dutifully throughout the event. They stood on a nearby pavement with an assortment of instruments that ranged from a set of drums to a violin. Ironically the appearance of their impromptu form of dress, tended to betray the musical talent that they all possessed.

With the lambs lying motionless on the ground, the farmers acted out a ritual dance in time to the music. The dance entailed the constant short shuffling of feet, in a forward direction, whilst encircling the surrounding area. The intention was to invoke the gods to smile favourably upon their lives and to give them a rich yield of livestock during the year that lay ahead.

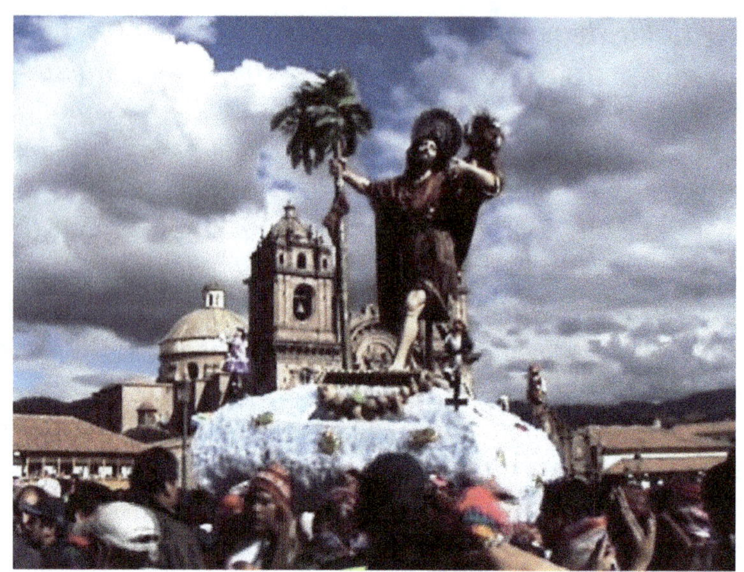

PHOTO NO 27
AN EFFIGY IN TRANSIT

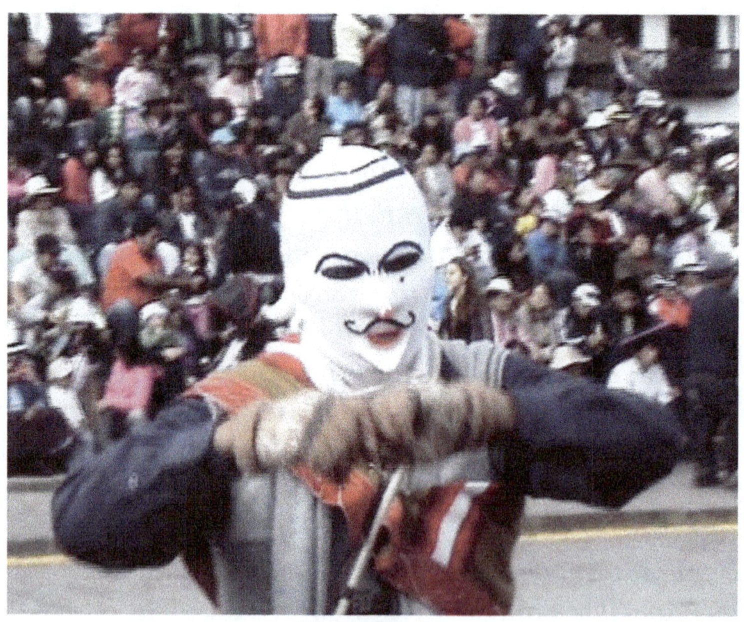

PHOTO NO 28
A FARMER PERFORMING AT CUSCO

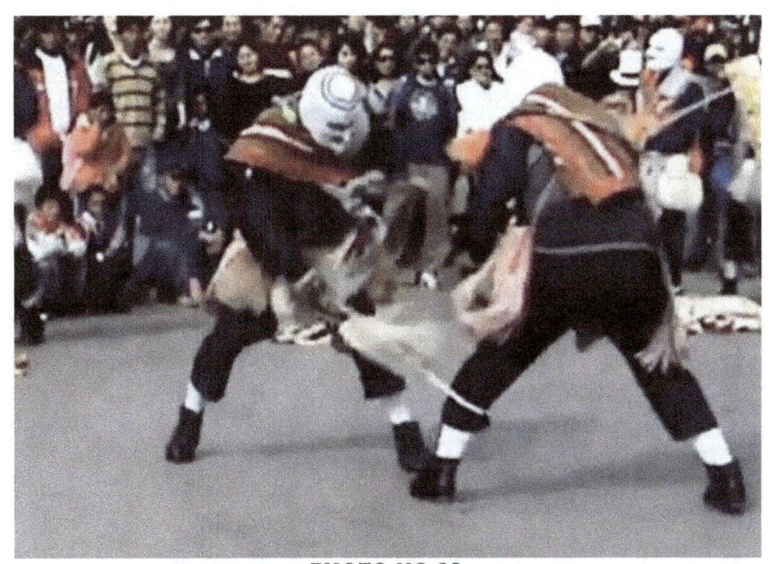

PHOTO NO 29
TWO FARMERS WITH WHIPS

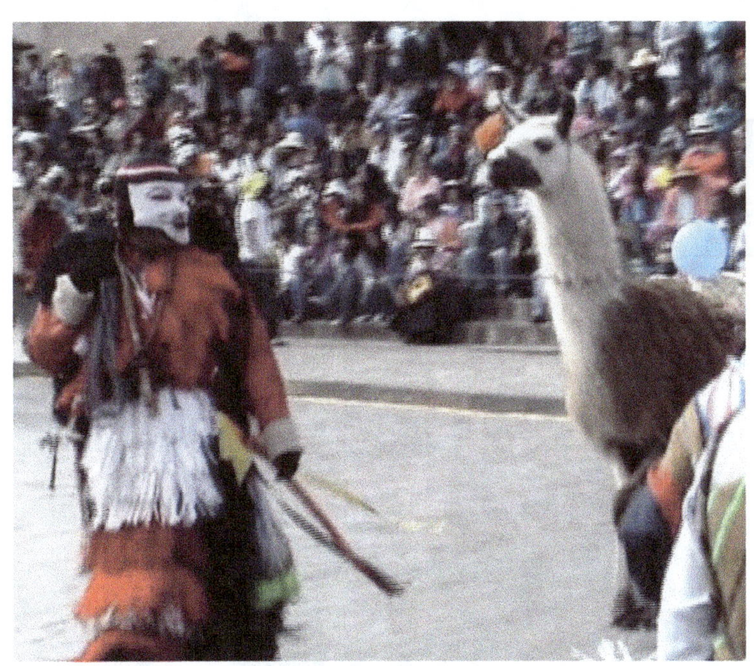

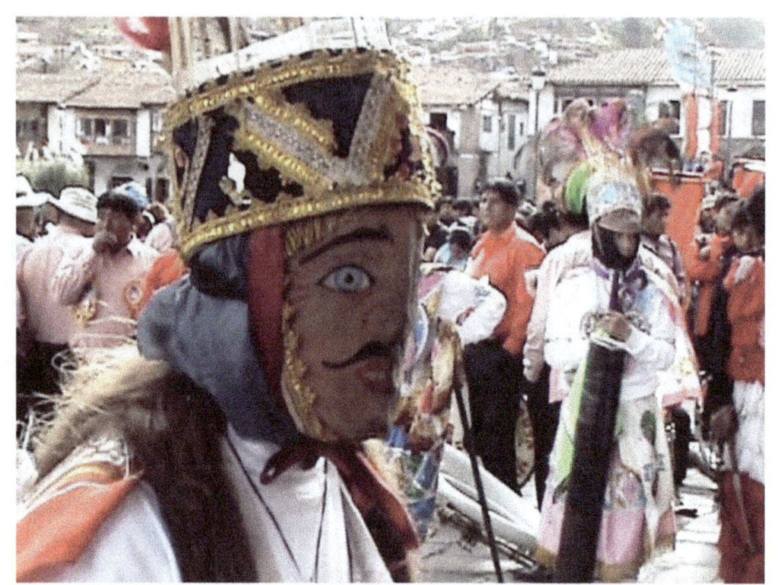

PHOTO NO 31
A FESTIVAL DANCER

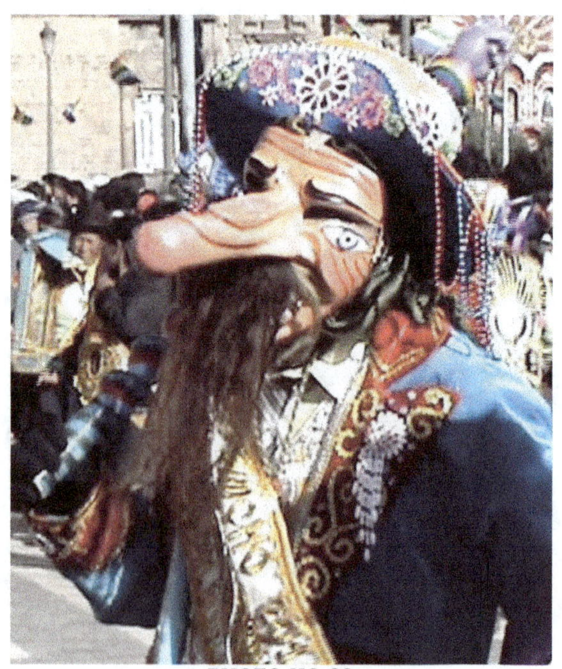

PHOTO NO 32
A FESTIVAL CHARACTER

It must be remembered that the Inca considered the natural elements to be deities and therefore to be feared and respected. Lightning in particular can have a devastating effect upon livestock and so the deity of lightning had to be appeased. During the ritual, pairs of farmers took hold of whips and in sympathy with the music, began to lash each other's lower legs. The sound of the whips cracking against the victims' legs is considered to simulate that which is made by the crack of lightning. The pace of whipping increased as the pace of the music stepped up. Finally, as a crescendo was reached, the music stopped abruptly. Instantly the protagonists fell prostrate to the ground. The crowds loved the action and the sounds from peals of laughter, with rounds of applause, reverberated in the air. There were other characters involved in this pageant and not least a pseudo 'rainbow' and an actual llama.

The third part of the day's festivities was performed by a body of dancers. They were men dressed in garb that identified with that of ancient Inca warriors. Their costumes were colourful and gay to the extreme. A headdress of feathers gave the impression of regality. A muslin mask with painted-on face, afforded the wearer an assumed identity. Leggings were worn under a kind of kilted skirt, whilst a colourful silk cape was draped over their shoulders. Polished lightweight leather shoes, afforded the dancers the ease of movement that they needed to perform their dance routines.

Once again a bespoke band played in sympathy to the dancers' agile movements. Instruments made from brass, that included a pair of large hand held cymbals, provided the tempo that was required to match the agility of the fleet-footed performers. Two parallel lines of costumed pseudo warriors, faced each other with upraised sticks. They moved forwards in a skipping fashion and clashed their sticks lightly together. In a smooth flowing movement they swivelled around and returned to their starting positions. Having regrouped, by once again standing in parallel lines, they repeated the sequence again and again. And all of this in time to the music.

Later in the afternoon lots of different performers gathered in the square. They wore a collection of themed costumes. Whilst using the medium of mime, they acted out scenes of historical events from the annals of the Inca's history.

All in all the day's events proved to be both spectacular and thoroughly enjoyable. When the displays eventually came to an end and the public started to disperse, I reluctantly made my way back to the hotel.

At the reception desk, I was given something I had not expected to see. It was a message in the form of a paper note. It stated that the next morning a bus would collect me from the hotel. At 0620hrs. it would take me to a railway station and from there I would travel by train to Machu Picchu, the Sacred City of the Incas. The note also stated that there would be a 'phone call to my room an hour before departure. That was to make sure I was ready in time for the journey.

It was nice to know that the tour company were clearly taking care of every step of my holiday.

MACHU PICCHU
∗∗∗∗∗∗∗∗∗∗∗∗

It was an early start on the morning of June the ninth. I was out of bed at 0520hrs. I washed and dressed then dashed off to the dining room for a quick breakfast. With everything 'done and dusted', as the saying goes, I went to the hotel foyer. There I waited in advance of a coach that arrived at around 0620hrs. The journey to the railway station took just on thirty minutes to get there. The station was nothing more than a dot on the map. It went by the name of 'Poroy' which is derived from the expression, "For today, we stay here." That might have been alright for whoever named it but I for one planned to be on my way as soon as possible. The station's entrance area was buzzing with tourists. They were waiting to make the momentous journey to the piece de resistance of Peruvian tours. It was of course the magnificent archaeological site of Machu Picchu.

The station itself looked to be many years old but aside from that it was kept in fine condition and was spotlessly clean. There was an entrance area that was closed off from the railway platform. Through the windows of its locked doors, I could see the locomotive with its train of carriages. Resplendent in its appearance, it stood on rails and waited like some thoroughbred race horse about to be exercised. Long polished wooden benches, were provided for the waiting travellers. They could sit on them to rest their weary limbs. Coffee and tea was for available to refresh one's palate. Once again, the organisation of the Peruvian authorities, together with the tour company I was employing, showed themselves to be working at their best.

I was handed three paper vouchers that authorised the whole adventure. The first was to give me passage from Poroy station to Machu Picchu. The second was to allow me to return. The outward train journey terminated at a small but well developed area close to Machu Picchu. It went by the name of Aguas Calientes. The third voucher provided for bus transport. It was to take me from a designated boarding point at Aguas Calientes, to the historical site of Machu Picchu.

Curiously all three tickets had my name printed on them along with an allocated seat number. But surprisingly there was also a carriage number of the train! How efficient is that? However, for some reason that remains obscure to me, the third voucher was printed with the additional information of my age, sex and country of origin.

Just after 0700hrs the doors of the entrance area were unlocked and the travellers allowed to board the train. Of course that was after the staff had inspected their travel vouchers. Finding my allocated seat was effortless since everything was clearly marked. The seating was arranged in pairs and faced towards each other. A fixed functional table occupied the space in-between them. Comfort was paramount and space more than adequate. In addition to this, the carriages were built to provide for maximum visibility. Windows were placed, not only in the walls but even in the roof area! Since a good portion of the journey was flanked by tall mountains, the roof windows allowed for excellent views. They also served to maximise the available daylight.

A young couple sat opposite to me, who as I discovered had travelled from Australia to make the journey. I also discovered that the male member of the duo had plenty to talk about. We engaged in conversation for most of the three and a half hour journey!

At one end of the carriage I could see a small area that was equipped for serving refreshments.

It was also fitted with a built-in bar top and was manned by two uniformed staff members. Opposite to this useful feature was a sizeable washroom that was provided with a toilet. After about an hour of travelling the two uniformed gents walked down the aisle. Each passenger received from them a complimentary drink, a packet of sliced dried-banana chips and two chocolate biscuits.

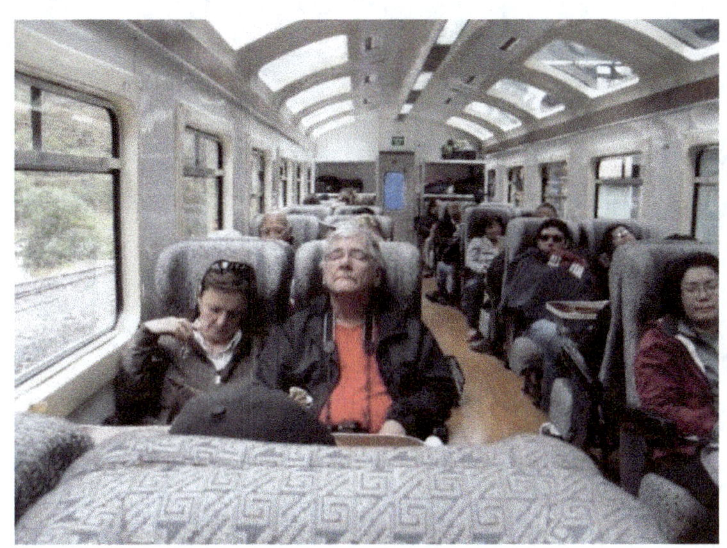

PHOTO NO 33
ON THE TRAIN TO AGUAS CALIENTES

Of course further refreshments could be purchased on request. The train travelled parallel to the Rio Urubamba (Urubamba River) that was flanked by mountainous cliffs and peaks. The surrounding scenery was spectacular and was akin to watching a colourful moving canvas that had been painted by a master artist. At about sixty-seven kilometres from the starting point, the train stopped at a station called Ollantaytambo. It shared its name with a small village that had been an ancient Inca resting place. Today there were no Incas to be seen.

But as I looked through the carriage window, I could make out a large number of back packers who were setting out to walk the 'Inka Trail.'

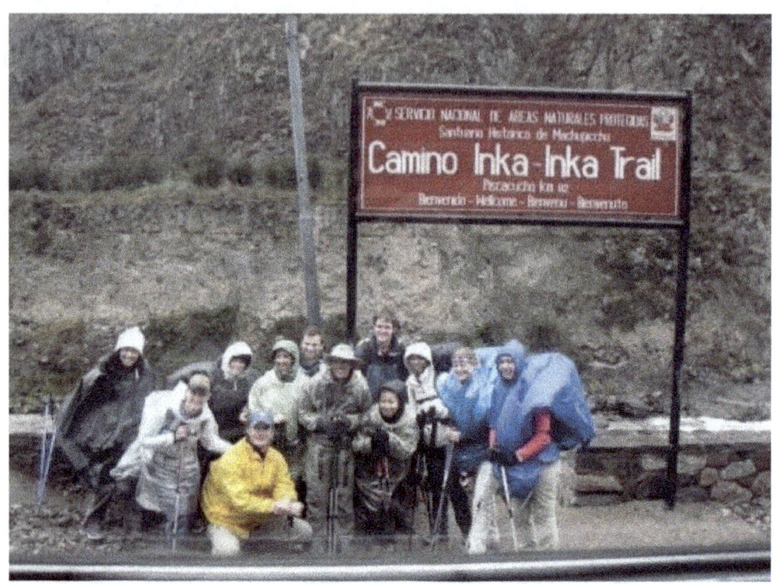

PHOTO NO 34
BACK PACKERS AT THE START OF THE INKA TRAIL

They were at the starting point of a four day and three night hike. It would take them along the route known as the 'Classic Inka Trail.' In total it is forty-five kilometres in length. They would be following in the ancient footsteps of the Incas. The trail would require them to cross bridges and to climb hills. In one particular place, they would descend the thousand stone steps of a stairway. It would eventually reach the citadel of Machu Picchu.

Gazing upon their smiling faces I thought about the hardship they would have to endure. A feeling of smugness overcame me, knowing that I would arrive at the famous site before them. But more importantly, in far greater comfort!

****

THE INCA POPULATION

The Incas rose to power during the 1400's and like most successful civilisations they built an extensive road system much of which is still visible today. As well as roads they left other evidence that demonstrated that they were master engineers and builders. This was in the form of stone built cities that rivalled those of ancient Rome. However, unlike the Romans they managed to achieve all this without the use of the wheel, iron tools or even a written language. At any rate that is what archaeologists believe. They may not have had a written language either but they did have an ingenious system that used various lengths of knotted string. The strings were anchored together at one end, rather like a bunch of keys on a key ring. Each strand of string had a combination of knots tied in them. The knots would be tied in a variety of ways and the strings would vary in colour. Collectively these were known as 'Kiphus' or 'Quipus. The information they contained could be carried over great distances by runners, to be interpreted some time later by a knowledgeable recipient.

In addition to having these skills, the Incas were efficient warriors who subjugated dozens of different peoples and forged them into one of the largest Empires in the world. The fortress or citadel of Machu Picchu sits on a mountainous saddle that joins two tall mountains. The larger of the two is named Machu Picchu, which means 'Old Mountain' because of its size. Similarly, the smaller mountain is called Huayna Picchu or 'Young Mountain' and once again due to its size. Huayna Picchu is the one that normally features in most photographs of the site whilst Machu Picchu is usually located behind the camera. The complex which takes its name from the 'Old Mountain' is situated in the highland jungle at an altitude of 2432m (7972 feet) so it is possible to feel altitude sickness. Therefore visitors are advised to carry a bottle of water with them. The most common stone found in the region is greyish-white granite which contains high quantities of quartz, mica, and feldspar thus making it relatively easy to shape. Because of these attributes, the rock was a magnificent building material for the Inca masons. Machu Picchu was principally used as a ceremonial site and only an estimated thousand or so people actually lived there at any given time. These were comprised of the Royalty, priests, and numerous workers.

They were fed by transforming the steep slopes of the mountain into terraces that were used as productive farmland. Archaeologists believe that more land was under cultivation at the time of the Incas, than there is today in modern Peru. Surprisingly, in view of all this, the Inca only ruled for one hundred years after which their Empire was decimated. First by disease, then by civil war and finally by the Spanish Conquistadores. By the time of the Spanish conquest of Cusco in 1534, Machu Picchu was largely abandoned and thus drew little attention from the Spaniards. The roads leading to it became overgrown and so too did the buildings, leaving the entire site lost to the world for centuries. That is until 1914, when an American explorer named Hiram Bingham found his way to the ruins and declared their presence to the archaeological world.

ARRIVAL AT AGUAS CALIENTES

At the end of the three and a half hour journey, the train came to a halt at a stopping point called Aguas Calientes. Due to my improved Spanish I understood the name to mean 'Hot Waters'. I followed the travellers as they disembarked from the train. Buses waited to transport us to the top of the mountain range.

The area that surrounds the railway station is sizeable. It has a conglomeration of souvenir shops and hotels that have sprung up alongside the Rio Urubamba. Towering high above this hive of activity is the majestic looking Machu Picchu. It seems to be keeping a watchful eye on the events unfolding at its base.

The rail track upon which I had travelled, was soon exchanged for a tarred road. Along this road a bus wound its way up the rocky terrain. After a few minutes the bus stopped. It had reached the top of the mountain road and was parked next to a building having toilets and refreshment facilities. There was also a shop from where souvenirs could be bought.

Stepping off the bus I was greeted by yet another friendly guide who identified herself to me and three others in our party. The formalities of inspecting our tour vouchers was completed and we walked towards the entrance to the historical site. Along the way I noticed a small makeshift office. People were queuing to have their passports franked with a special rubber stamp. It had the words, 'Machu Picchu' embossed on it. Thinking this to be a nice idea by way of providing a little proof that I had been there, I joined the queue. Afterwards our small group walked the last few metres before reaching the spectacle of the Inca stronghold.

At this juncture it may be worth mentioning that there are certain restrictions in place for some senior citizens. The use of walking sticks is limited to people who actually need to use them. To prove that one does, a medical certificate would need to be shown at the time of entry. For wheelchair users there is a further restriction. It is only possible to reach a limited area of the site. There is also a restriction on the use of umbrellas. Large ones with metal points are not allowed whilst only small foldaway types are acceptable.

Rain can fall at unpredictable times and hence the need for an umbrella. However, the local shops do a brisk trade in selling a foldaway poncho-style rain coat. One can be bought for the equivalent of five Pounds Sterling. Following our guide along a well defined stone path we were obliged to squeeze through a couple of stone doorways, at the same time avoiding contact with tourists. They were making their way towards us having finished their exploration of the ruins. As we entered through a second stone doorway and into the viewing area, suddenly the scene blossomed like a newly opened flower.

It provided the glorious sight of the stone ruins that I had for so long desired to see. It was a surreal feeling. All the photographs I had seen in magazines and on the internet were now banished into oblivion. They made way for the tangible image that was present before my eyes. I was thrilled beyond description and gazed in awe. Of course, for our guide it was just another day, having seen the same sight time and again. Nevertheless she rose to the occasion and offered to take my photograph with a view of the ruins behind me.

For over two hours she escorted our party around the site whilst showing us the various points of interest. At one end of the location stood a stone slab, which was mounted vertically into the ground. Its upper edge was shaped to match that of a mountain range, which looked on it from a great distance across the valley. It has been dubbed 'The Sacred Rock.' It is claimed that the Incas imitated natural forms, such as mountains, that they considered to be sacred. In another area of the site sat two stone circular dishes that were let into the ground. Each measuring about two feet in diameter they could be filled with water. Their practical use is open to conjecture but my favourite suggestion is that whilst filled with *water, they would reflect the image of stars in the night sky. The priests could then use them as 'water mirrors' to observe the celestial objects in relative comfort. [See Photo No 38]*

Our party was guided to the 'Temple of the Condor' where a huge cut stone lay on the ground. It represented the head and neck of the revered bird. Whilst rising up behind it, an enormous rocky outcrop looked like the bird's wings in full flight. Afterwards we were shown a subterranean cavern where it is thought that human sacrifice may have taken place. Later we saw the 'Intihuatana' which is a large stone sculpture. It has a stepped base that stands almost two metres in height and a singular central column that is seventy centimetres high. It is highly probable that it was used for astronomical purposes.

During our visit we saw that many of the buildings had trapezoidal shaped windows and doorways. In particular the walls of the Main Temple within the complex, had some seventeen niches of a trapezoidal shape built into them. They were so shaped in order to withstand any earthquakes that posed a constant potential threat in the region.

It was at the Main Temple that our little group stopped to rest and to listen to information offered by our guide. We sat on a row of stones that faced an outside wall of the building. At the time, I was wearing my sun glasses, which I think may have had some polarizing effect on the light. During the talk I believe I saw a faded painted image on the temple wall. It looked to me like a full-size puma with curved tail that was standing upright and with its head pointing in the direction of the priests' house. When I took my glasses off it wasn't visible. I told the guide of my sighting but she smiled and shrugged it off. Who knows if perhaps there was an outline on the stone work that was rendered visible due to the right lighting condition?

At the end of her talk, our guide explained that in the next half hour, a bus would return us to the base of the mountain. Until then we were free to explore on our own. The way I saw it, there wasn't a lot that could be done in half an hour and so I ambled slowly towards the exit. Along the way I marvelled at the sights of that magical place. At one section I chanced to see a llama that trotted about quite unconcerned by the intrusion of human visitors. More or less at the same time, I noticed a young woman who was also watching the animal. I said hello and we started a conversation. I quickly learned she had travelled from Argentina to be there.

Fulfilling the guide's promise, the bus took me to the base of the mountain. It stopped close to a restaurant that was built next to the Rio Urubamba. Inside the restaurant a meal awaited me and the cost of it was included in the Viator itinerary. It was basically a help yourself buffet but was sufficient to see me through the following three and a half hour train journey. Based upon the outward journey, I had an idea of what to expect and wondered who would be my new travelling companions. This time I was sat opposite two young Canadians. Shortly before the train set off we started talking. We didn't stop again until we reached Poroy railway station!

After the train journey I arrived at the Hotel Mabey by 2100hrs and was greeted by the receptionist. He presented me with another paper telephone message. It stated that at 0920hrs the next morning, a coach would arrive to ferry me to the airport. From there I would make my return journey to Lima. The time of departure was welcomed news. The later collection time meant I could have a little longer in bed; or so I thought!

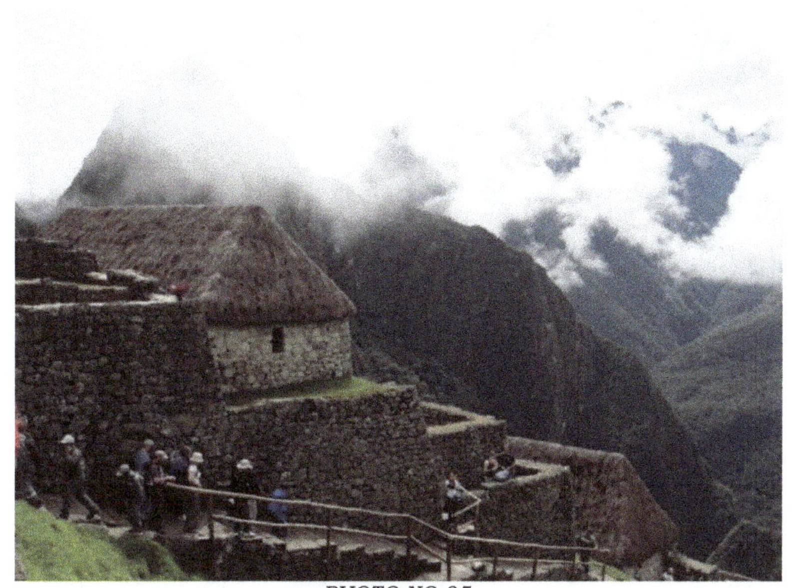

PHOTO NO 35
CLOUD SWIRLING AROUND THE RUINS AT MACHU PICCHU

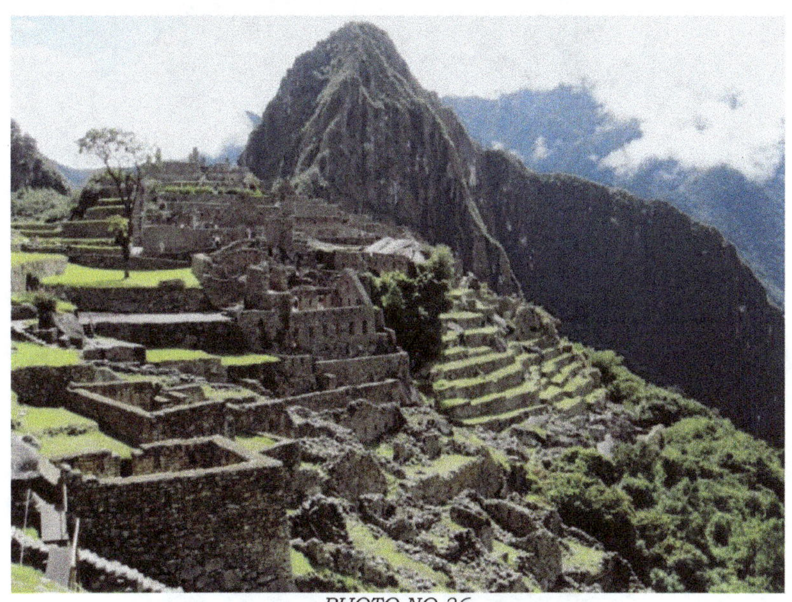

PHOTO NO 36
THE RUINS AND HUAYNA PICCHU

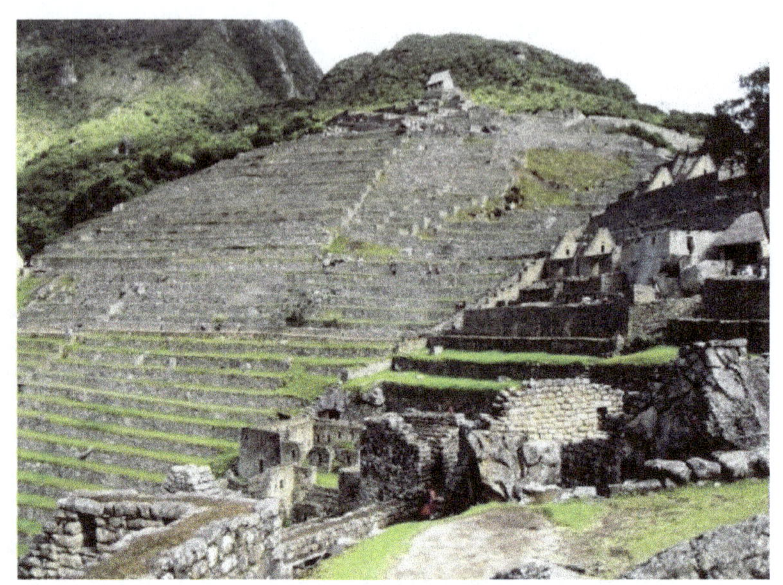

PHOTO NO 37
TIERED TERRACES IN FRONT OF MACHU PICCHU

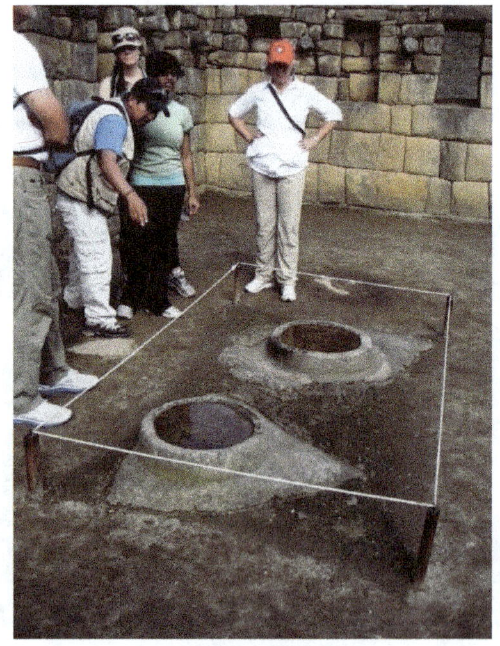

PHOTO NO 38
BOWLS OF WATER

FLYING FROM CUSCO TO LIMA

On the morning of June the tenth I was aroused by the sound of loud voices and the banging of suitcases outside my room. A contingent of Chinese people had just arrived at the hotel. In my semi comatose state, I reasoned they would soon go to the dining room to eat breakfast. Delaying as long as possible, I walked into the dining room an hour later. The people were still seated at their tables and sounding like a gathering of battery hens!

At the one vacant table I sat and ate my food. As I swallowed the last mouthful the crowd finally began to disperse. Whilst sipping a cup of hot tea, my glazed eyes looked through a window towards the distant mountains. I mused over the experiences I had enjoyed during my visit to Cusco. My last breakfast in the ancient Inca capital was finished. Making my way down the hotel's darkened staircase, I intended to return to my room. The lighting was none too bright and as I rounded the foot of the stairwell, something white in colour caught my attention. Doing a quick half turn, I saw two black-clothed figures seated on a couple of suitcases. At first glance I thought they might be spectres. In reality the figures were Chinese people dressed totally in black. They wore of all things, white face masks! The masks were of the type that are worn in China, as a protection against air pollution. Staring in disbelief I wondered if they might be ninjas! Suddenly the couple both raised a hand and waved to me. It was like a magical spell had been broken. I returned the gesture but the incident had given me quite a start. Later, after regaining my composure, I saw the humour in it all. I thought to myself, "I know the hotel is far from perfect, but to wear anti-pollution masks, was surely taking things to the extreme!"

On arrival at Cusco airport a tour guide escorted me to the check-in desk and placed my suitcase onto the weigh scale. Speaking in Spanish, the check-in lady bid me good day and asked to see my passport. The guide, who was standing to one side, quickly informed her that I was English speaking. She instantly apologised and spoke to me in English, as she continued to prepare my boarding pass. All the time a couple of men wearing plain clothes stood behind her. They were watching us intently. Slowly they sidled up to the weigh scale. One of them stretched out his hand to touch the orange-coloured plastic bag. The one that was tied to the handle of my suitcase.

The reader will recall from my earlier writing, that the plastic bag was a means for me to identify the case more readily at the reclaim centre.

Lightly tugging at the bag, the man's eyes looked up and locked on to mine. He gave the hint of a smile, to which I responded in like manner. It crossed my mind that he saw some humour in my little decoration. I must confess it did seem amusing for the first time, having put aside the serious practicality of the bag. Without appearing fazed and not arousing my suspicion, the man slowly moved from the case and edged closer to the check-in lady. A few whispered words were exchanged. Then suddenly and unexpectedly, he pulled from his pocket what looked like a leather wallet. It was attached to a lanyard that hung around his neck. Like a striking cobra, he thrust the leather object forward towards my face. With its lanyard straining under the tension, I saw the piece of leather displayed a brass shield-shaped badge. The word 'POLICE' was boldly embossed upon it. It was all so surreal. It seemed like I had been instantly placed into a scene from a Hollywood crime movie. With a speed matching that of his hand movement, his voice uttered the words, "I'm from the Interior Police Department, would you follow me! I want to inspect your suitcase!" The badge of authority was immediately replaced into his pocket. In a swift follow-up movement he dragged my suitcase away and into an adjoining room. A strange noise began to fill my ears. I instantly realized it was the sound of my knees. They were knocking! I was terrified!

After striding over the weigh scales and moving passed the check-in lady, I followed the two men into the screening room. One asked to see my passport whilst the other asked for the key to open the suitcase. Before I could say, "Hasta La Vista Baby," that is assuming I might have been given the opportunity to do so, my suitcase was opened and laid prostrate on the floor. The policeman's hands began probing amongst my clothing. Like some over anxious pervert he prodded and poked into every area he could find.

In the meantime the man with my passport scrutinised every page. Questions were fired at me as if his mouth was some kind of gun. "Did you pack your own suitcase?" "Where are you going?" "Where have you been?" "What kind of work do you do?" Meanwhile the man, who was seemingly groping the contents of my suitcase, appeared to be looking for something specific. He didn't remove any article from the case but he did inspect the lining. The passport man, apparently satisfied with his inspection, cast his attention in the direction of his colleague but more precisely towards my suitcase. He had spotted an electrical cable, which was one that I use when charging the battery of my video camera. He brought it to the attention of his colleague. An expression from his eyes suggested it might have some sinister application. Thankfully his idea was quashed by whom I think was the senior man.

He simply looked and shook his head. The passport man was momentarily taken aback by this rebuff and within a minute or two my case was being closed.

During the zipping process I introduced a sudden change of mood when I uttered the words, "Uno momento por favor". (One minute please) Both officials stiffened, as if to expect some revelation that might satisfy their quest. Crouching next to the senior man, my hands moved the end of the zipper and the little padlock that secured it, closer to the end carrying handle. I explained my action with the words, "por protection". That was where I assumed there would be less chance of them being damaged. The senior man acknowledged my gesture while the other stood silent and continued looking perplexed. Seconds later I was told I could go and was wished a "nice journey."

I was never more gladdened to be leaving an airport in my life!

My 'plane was about to leave. With quaking body and molested case, I hurried towards the boarding gate as fast as I could. Of course, I didn't know at the time but Lima is considered to be the drugs capital of the world!

RETURN TO MIRAFLORES

Whilst enjoying the comfort of wide leather seats, the flight over the snow-capped Andes Mountains, was both pleasant and free from any turbulence. When the aeroplane landed at Lima airport my pre-paid Peruvian tour was officially over. No guides were there to greet me or to carry my case. No one to ferry me to and from hotels. From now onwards I had to fend for myself.

The guide books recommended taking an official taxi at any airport, so as not to be duped. They were considered to be a little more expensive than others, but in the long run would prove to be cost effective. As I walked into the airport concourse I felt and probably looked vulnerable. But I soon spotted a man who was clearly a taxi driver. He was smartly dressed and spoke good English. I asked him for identification and without hesitation he produced an official card. Afterwards he pointed out a licence that was displayed on his taxi. This time it was I who was checking documentation!

The formalities appeared and felt to be right and so we drove off in the direction of Miraflores. We arrived at my pre-booked hotel that went by the name of Wasi Independencia.

Prior to booking my Viator trip I had looked on line for accommodation and had found the Wasi Independencia. From the outside the onlooker would be forgiven for thinking that the place was just an ordinary house. It was placed amidst a row of properties in a side street. Tall white washed walls stood on either side of a locked entrance door. Twenty-four hour security was provided which meant that an intercom was provided to gain access. Once the narrow front door was opened it seemed like stepping into Dr Who's Tardis. There was an open forecourt with tables and chairs, which I later discovered was where guests would eat their breakfast.

Beyond this area was a reception desk and behind it a singular staircase. The latter ascended to two upper floors having a series of bedrooms. My room had a large single bed and next to it was a card table and a stand chair. A small but adequate TV monitor was attached to a wall and there was a singular window allowing daylight to enter.

Separated by a sliding screen was a small shower room having a toilet and wash basin. Evidently the water in Lima is not chlorinated as in European cities. Therefore it is best not to drink tap water. Also the sewage systems are not of the best. Because of this, plastic containers are kept next to the water closet. The idea being to deposit used paper into the container and not to flush it down the loo.

Noticeably there was an absence of shelves, cupboards and wardrobes in my room. This resulted in my suitcase having to substitute for all three roles. In fact everything was basic but functional. In any event it was regularly cleaned.

RETURN TO LIMA CITY

It was June the eleventh and I decided to spend the day in central Lima. At least that was my intention but first of all I had to find my way there. English was not widely spoken in the areas I visited. Even most of the information signs, such as the ones inside the museums, were mostly printed in Spanish. Fortunately my hotel receptionist spoke reasonable English. I asked her what would be the best way of getting to Lima. In a word, 'Metropolitano' was her answer. Her English left me unsure about how this mode of transport functioned. But the word 'Metropolitano' conjured up the idea of an underground rail system. I assumed it would be well sign posted and fairly straight forward to use.

It turned out not to be a rail system but rather a glorified bus service. But having said that, I was about to discover it was a service that was well thought out.

'Donde esta?' are valuable Spanish words to learn. They mean 'Where is?' If you want to find somewhere, just add the name of where you are going onto the end of the phrase. In my case, 'Donde esta Metropolitano?' did the trick. Each person I asked got me closer to the boarding point of the nearest Metropolitano station. Very soon I found myself facing a turnstile. But it prevented my entry to the platform. Some nearby machines demanded money in exchange for a travel ticket. Unfortunately I couldn't understand the instructions. As people arrived at the station logic dictated that I should ask someone to help me operate a machine. A young man was my first victim and he tried his best to help. Sadly, his English was not good enough for me to understand what I must do. He had to leave in a hurry. I felt stranded like a beached whale, although hopefully not looking as big!

To my surprise and instant joy a young senorita appeared. She took up the challenge. She made me understand that I needed to place money into the machine in exchange for a plastic card. Rather like a bank card it would be valid for my return trip to Lima. Giving her some Soles she quickly operated the mechanical wonder and produced a card. Then, like a school teacher taking a pupil on a day outing, she proceeded to show me how to open the turnstile. We descended a flight of steps. Standing on a platform we exchanged a few words. Hers in broken English and mine in fractured Spanish! We waited for what I thought might be a train. As I looked around it seemed strange to me that there were no rails. Instead there was a well defined concrete driveway. It had high concrete sides and was open to the sky.

It was a professional bus lane that catered for a twin-carriage single-decker bus. When one arrived it drew up alongside the edge of the raised platform. The bus was well patronized and when inside I hung on to a nearby safety pole. The bus sped along and my new found friend gave me periodic updates on our whereabouts. In the interim, a tug on my jacket sleeve revealed the presence of a senora. She was a senior person like myself. She offered her seat for me to sit down. I was bowled over by this show of respect and thanked her as best I could. But at the same time declined the offer.

After a few minutes, my young friend made a special effort to make sure I saw the Lima football stadium. Perhaps she thought that since I came from England I must be a football fan. Very soon the bus glided to a halt. It was my stop. Thanking the senorita profusely I stepped off the bus and into the great unknown. A smiling face and a waving hand was the last I saw of her.

Facing me was a large building that looked like a bus station. It had many passageways and numerous stairways. There were plenty of signs but the Spanish names printed on them held little meaning for me. I decided to follow a small group of people who appeared to be heading for the outside. Sure enough they were. I found myself standing on the main street of 'de la Union.' Convincing myself there was a certain method in my apparent madness, I proceeded to look for Lima's Museum of Archaeology. But to find my way there was another matter.

Immediately I was accosted by a man who wanted to clean my shoes! He carried with him all the accoutrements for the job. They included jars of polish and a wooden stool on which to place my foot. I hastily brushed him away (pardon the pun) as I was intent on finding my goal. He persisted and followed close behind me as I hurried along. When I approached a road junction having a set of traffic lights, I watched as they were about to change colour. Just when they changed in my favour, I rushed across the street. The action left my pursuer stranded on his side of the road. Realising his dilemma he finally gave up the chase. Later that day, my conscience pricked me like a thorn. I felt increasingly sorry for the man but what was done was done.

Nearby was a building having a sign that surprisingly was written in English. It read, 'Info Peru Tourist Information.' To me this seemed akin to a genie appearing from a magical lamp and granting me a wish. The building was old and must have had a previous use. Today, one of its rooms was occupied by a team of ladies. They appeared as busy as honey bees, whilst tapping away on their computer key boards. One of them presently stood up and addressed me. She said, "Hello I'm Laura Lopez can I help you?" I explained that I was hoping to find directions to the Museum of Archaeology. She informed me that it was quite a distance away but offered to find a map for me to use.

As she was looking for the map I chanced to see a brochure. It advertised various coach tours for both in and around Lima. One of them took my fancy. It was an organised visit to an ancient temple complex known as Pachacamac. It was not too far from where I lived and it boasted one or more adobe pyramids.

When I inquired about the tour, Laura said I could make a booking both there and then. Furthermore, a tour was available for the following day. It seemed like the wheel of good fortune was turning nicely in my favour. Without hesitation I made the booking, paid the fee and collected my ticket. All in the space of a few minutes.

The collection point for the Pachacamac tour was to be outside the Hotel Doubletree El Pardo. Fortuitously it stood on the corner of the street where my accommodation was based. I asked myself, "Could it get any better?"

The immediate task that faced me was how I was going to find the Museum at Lima. Laura advised me not to walk to the Museum due to the distance and also the possible risk of meeting the odd felon. Instead she asked, "Have you used Peru's taxis yet?" Apart from the one that initially ferried me from the airport to my hotel I had to answer "No".

"Well, let me show you" she said and beckoned me to follow her to the street. As if by some pre-arranged plan, a car that looked vaguely like a taxi, approached us from the top end of the street. She flagged it down and the car stopped. A few sentences of Spanish were exchanged and within seconds I found myself sitting in the back of the taxi. It headed for the sought after Museum. But not before thanking Laura for all her help.

She was right about the distance. It was a fair drive to the Museum through the sprawling city of Lima. But the journey gave me an opportunity to take in some of the less publicised sites of the metropolis. At the same time I could observe the general public and thus gain a better understanding of Peruvian life.

The Museo Nacional de Arqueologia, Antropologia e Historia del Peru, is a wonderfully well preserved building. It stands on the Plaza Bolivar in the district of Pueblo Libre. Essentially it is a single storey construction set out in the form of an oblong. The central part of the building has a large area of grass, which resembles a lawn. Facing each of its four sides are cloisters having numerous archways.

The archways rest on a wide, wooden-floored corridor. This in turn skirts the many large rooms, that house the museum's fascinating artefacts. I found myself spending most of the day looking at the numerous and varied objects. Collectively they attempt to explain to the onlooker, the social history of this part of the world. To complement the experience there was a well equipped snack bar. The contents of which kept me periodically refreshed. There was also a number of staff members who were incredibly obliging. At the end of the visit I quickly found a taxi outside the museum's entrance. My previously acquired knowledge was put into practice and I negotiated a fare to take me directly to Miraflores.

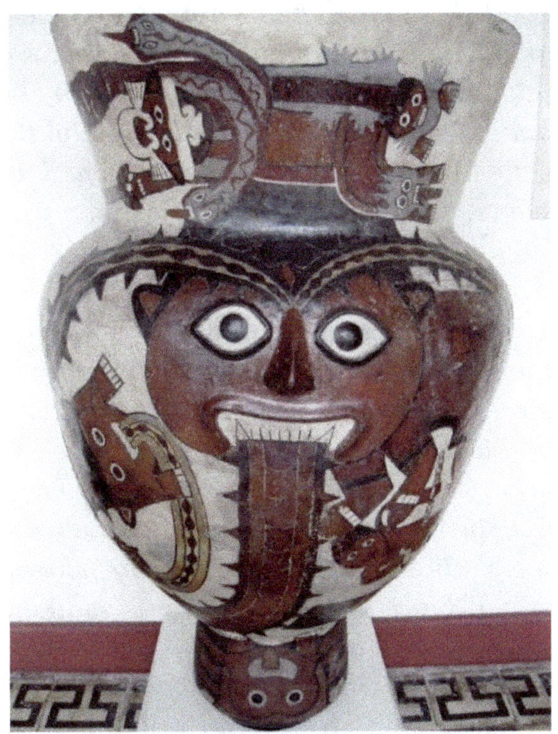

PHOTO NO 39
A WATER CONTAINER AT THE LIMA MUSEUM

115

BARRANCO
****

June the twelfth was another sunny day and another adventure awaited me. I was due to visit the temple of the oracle, at the historic Pachacamac complex.

Sitting at one of the hotel's tables, in the shade cast by a large umbrella, I slowly consumed my breakfast. Although somewhat repetitive the food was nonetheless tasty. It comprised of a starter in the form of a glass of orange juice and was closely followed by a bowl of mixed fruit. The latter tasted even better having liquid yogurt poured over it. Then a plate with three triangular shaped slices of ham and three similar slices of cheese was provided. To make these appear respectable, they were complemented by a small wicker basket containing three freshly baked bread rolls. Along with them was a small ceramic dish filled with butter. Finally, the piece de resistance to this visual feast was a small but freshly made omelette. After breakfast I sauntered to the end of the street to where my pick-up would arrive.

As a point of interest most of the streets in Peru have the prefix of 'ca' before the name. The 'ca' is an abbreviation of the Spanish word 'calle' which in English simply means 'street'. Along the streets are to be found apartment blocks. In Spanish they are known as 'cuadra.' They are numbered as say, 01, or 02, or 03 and so on. The numbering system makes it easier for finding one's direction of travel. By looking at the numbers it can be determined if one is walking towards an address or away from it.

The streets may be crossed by avenues, which in turn have their own name and the prefix of 'av.' Unfortunately there are no mandatory stop signs for any vehicle at the intersections. This results in motorists sounding their car horn to warn any approaching traffic.

It is all well and good for the drivers but the shrill sound can be most annoying for the average pedestrian.

True to form the coach arrived in good time. Climbing on board I was surprised to see that there were only three passengers plus our guide. Two of them were a middle-aged married couple. The third was a young senorita and all were from Peru. Our guide was a young Peruvian woman who looked fetching by wearing her three piece uniform. It comprised of a dark-blue coloured waistcoat with matching trousers. She also wore a pale-blue long-sleeved shirt. A dark-blue neckerchief was tied casually around her neck. Whilst her jet black hair and slender frame set her apart. In keeping with her appearance, she carried out her job with the upmost efficiency.

The coach wound its way along the streets of Miraflores passing the famous 'Parque del Amor' or 'The Park of Love'. The park is largely favoured by newlyweds. After their wedding ceremony, they gather there for photo shoots. In keeping with the theme of the park there is a sculptured monument that is dedicated to 'The Kiss'. Its creator is the Peruvian artist Victor Delfin.

The coach picked up the coastal road passing through the seaside resort of Chorrillos. It headed out towards the quaint district of Barranco. En route it stopped briefly at a spot along the coastline, to allow us to watch a most exciting spectacle. Looking down from our parking place we saw a precipitous rocky cliff. It was part of a peninsula that pointed towards the Pacific Ocean. Standing on the cliff and in full view of the many spectators, was a young man. He was clad in what appeared to be a monk's habit. From his stand point to the dashing sea below him was a drop of around a hundred feet or more. He was clearly about to dive into the sea. But beforehand he performed a short ritual. It added extra suspense to the unfolding drama.

Raising his arms wide apart and high above his head, he looked up to the sky. He appeared to be praying or at least seeking some form of spiritual help, in order to accomplish what he was about to do. After a few seconds his arms moved slowly downwards to his waist. Then, and quickly this time, he raised them again and in doing so leaned forward. Almost like watching a slow motion movie sequence, the man's body fell. It left the top of the cliff in an almost vertical dive towards the sea. There was a tremendous splash and the man disappeared momentarily beneath the surface of the waves. But just as quickly, he reappeared. He swam briefly towards the rocky cliff and found a place where he could haul himself from the water. He began his slow ascent by climbing stealthily up a natural stairway in the rocks.

Our coach driver waited long enough for the young man to reach us. His features suggested he must have been approaching his fortieth birthday. His half cupped hands further suggested he expected a monetary reward! After a little money changed hands the coach took off and only stopped again when we reached Barranco.

Originally founded by Spanish settlers, Barranco soon acquired the nickname of the 'City of Windmills.' Its early inhabitants frequently used windmills to draw water from the wells. Officially established in 1876, it became the second smallest of Lima's forty-three districts, whilst covering only 3,33 square kilometres. It wasn't long before Barranco proved to be the favourite beach resort of the wealthy families of Lima. Today it has numerous houses of a Colonial and Republican style that are known to the locals as 'casonas'. Beautiful flower-filled garden squares and litter free streets can be seen about its public places. Considered to be a home for poets, artists and photographers, Barranco is even a site of encounter for Bohemians. Apparently there are three understandings of the word Bohemian. The first refers to a resident of the former Kingdom of Bohemia; which is now known as the Czech Republic. Secondly, the meaning is derived from the French word, referring to 'gypsies,' or Romani people. Finally it denotes a socially unconventional person, especially one who is involved in the arts.

The district includes numerous restaurants, nightclubs, discos, bars and peñas. These are venues where one can appreciate Peruvian music. I must confess I didn't stay out late enough to sample the night life!

Barranco's beaches are among the most popular within the surfing community and a marina completed in the year 2008, provides state-of-the-art services for its well attended yacht club.

The name 'Barranco', which in English means 'ravine,' is descriptive of its topography. It is part of a cliff, overlooking a strip of sand, which stretches towards nearby Chorrillos. Incidentally, the cliffs of Chorrillos tend to shield Barranco from the cold and humid winds coming from the South. Because of this, Barranco has a micro-climate that is warmer and drier than many of the other districts of Lima. The others are generally more humid. Each side of the ravine is connected by a steel bridge. It is known as the 'Puente de los Suspiros' or 'Bridge of Sighs.' Although the bridge was built in 1876 it looks like it might have been erected yesterday.

Often frequented by courting couples the bridge was immortalized by the song of a local singer and composer named Isabel Larco.

But aside from all of this are two curious tales with which it is connected. The first has to do with a wealthy man's daughter who lived in one of the houses that are adjacent to the bridge.

So the story goes, the young lady fell in love with a lowly street sweeper. One has to presume that she may have caught sight of him one day, as he swept the nearby street. Then, perhaps they struck up a conversation. Anyway, the father must have thought that his daughter was more deserving of a wealthier suitor and as a result forbade the potential union of the couple.

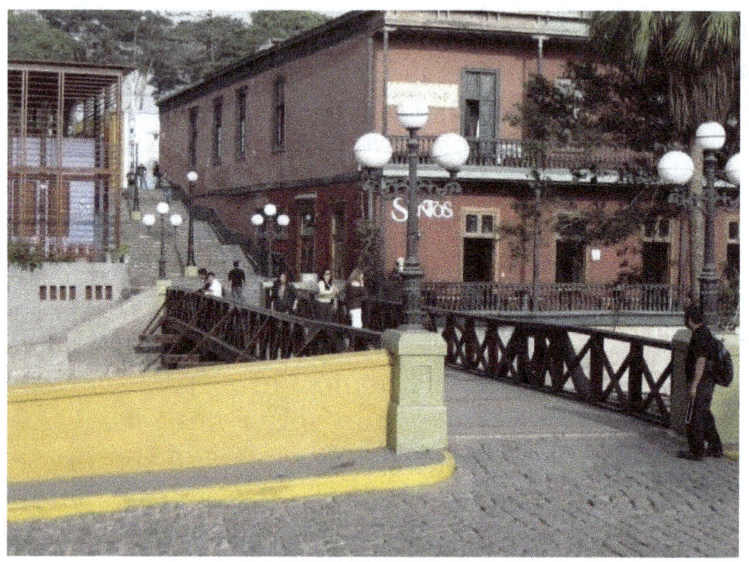

PHOTO NO 40
THE BRIDGE OF SIGHS

Sadly, the young damsel lived out her days as a spinster. She often waited at her window in the hope of catching a glimpse of her would-be paramour. It is said that those who walked across the bridge could hear her plaintive sighs.
The second tale is happier and is directed at anyone who sees the bridge for the first time. It is generally accepted that before crossing the bridge one must make a wish. Then after taking a deep breath, attempt to walk across it. If one completes the crossing without drawing a second breath, then the wish shall be granted.

Our tour guide had no further detail to add to this story. But having explained what she knew, we were unanimous in the decision to give it a go.

Our conveyance had stopped nearby and was parked next to a small garden area. We descended a flight of steps from the parking place. Passing the garden as we went, we approached the mouth of the bridge. Without any prompting our little group set off and almost in unison proceeded to cross. I had taken the obligatory deep breath and held it for all I was worth. I pushed forward towards my objective. The bridge is somewhat narrow and I found myself slightly hampered by a gentleman who was in front of me. Sadly he was obliged to walk with the aid of a walking stick which resulted in his pace being slower than mine. But to his credit he pushed on as fast as he could. Acting like some marathon runner I managed to overtake him but I was only to be met by a loving couple who were walking towards me. With desperation fast approaching I managed to squeeze passed them. Just as my mouth burst open and drew in a fresh supply of air, I had reached the other side! Seconds later the others followed suit. The mission had been accomplished. I for one qualified for my free wish but modesty prevents me from saying what I wished for.

Our guide walked us from the bridge to show us more of the nearby garden area. Besides a few trees and lots of colourful flowers, the garden boasted two bronze statues. One of them was a large figure of a long-haired woman, who wore a gown that touched the ground. Her face was tilted upwards towards the sky, with her arms outstretched in like manner. Some printed text on a bronze plaque, which was fixed to the supporting plinth, explained who the statue represented. It transpired that it was an effigy of one Maria Isabel Granda Larco who was a local singer and composer. At the start of her career her work was expressive and picturesque. It also evoked the romantic and beautiful neighbourhood of Barranco.

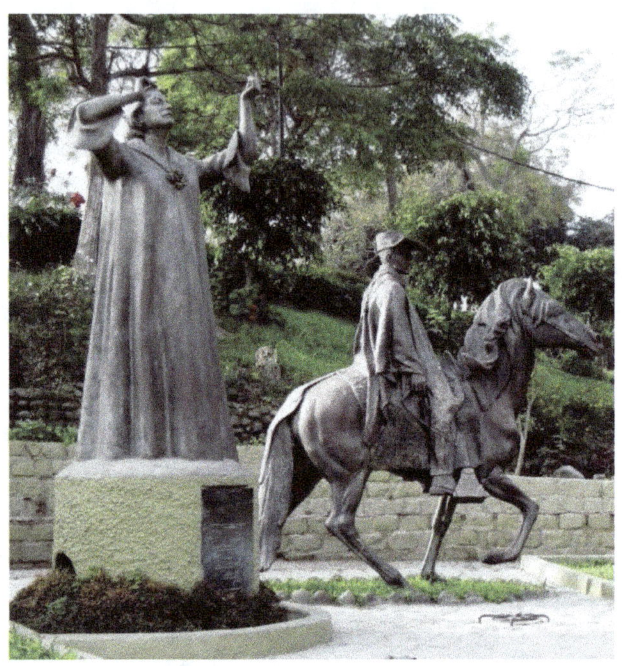

PHOTO NO 41
STATUES OF MARIA LARCO AND JOSE ANTONIO

Later on she composed a number of Creole waltzes having Afro-Peruvian rhythms. She also penned some well known songs of which are, "Lima de Veras", "La Flor de la Canela", (The Cinnamon Flower) "Fina Estampa", "Gracia", "José Antonio", and "Zeñó Manué".

She was more popularly known as Granda Larco and worked with a lengthy list of influential guitarists. These included Oscar Aviles, Lucho Garland, Lucho González, Alvaro Lagos, and Felix Casaverde.

Her song, "La Flor de la Canela" has become an anthem for the city of Lima, since in 1952, it was made popular by the Peruvian group 'Los Chamas.'

Rumour has it that there was a certain horseman called Jose Antonio, of whom she was particularly fond. It was he that she wrote a song about and gave it his name. The other bronze statue standing next to that of Granda Larco is of a man seated on a horse. It is said that this is meant to be an effigy of the same Jose Antonio.

Time had run out for the visit to Barranco and our little group were requested to return up the steps and to board our waiting transport. As we approached the coach it was hard to ignore an impressive looking church that towered above us. It is known by the name of Iglesia La Ermita. On one eventful night, according to a local legend, a group of fishermen were lost at sea, in Lima's famous dense winter fog. They prayed for salvation and miraculously a luminous cross appeared on land, guiding them back to shore. The Ermita church was built on the site where the cross allegedly appeared and since then has become the preferred church for fishermen. In the year 1881 the church was nearly destroyed by invading Chilean troops but has since been rebuilt and is an interesting site to visit.

PACHACAMAC TEMPLE

****

Our coach travelled for some minutes along the coastal road before arriving at the site of the Pachacamac Temple complex. The ruins are situated some forty kilometres south-east of Lima and nestle in the valley of the Lurin River. Built from adobe blocks, the temples and walls stretch across acres of land, presenting a breath taking sight. Pachacamac, whose name can be variously translated as 'He who Animated the World' or 'He who Created Land and Time', was the most important temple complex of the Andean coast.

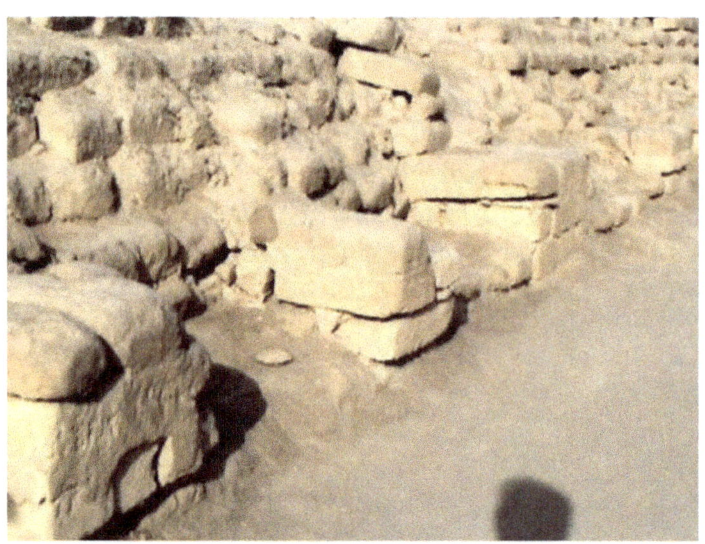

PHOTO NO 42
ADOBE SEATS AT THE PACHACAMAC TEMPLE

It functioned for more than 1500 years and was visited by multitudes of pilgrims. They attended religious ceremonies whilst seeking the aid of its reputed powers. At the main temple, which was built in the form of an enormous adobe step pyramid, was an 'oracle' that was used to predict the future. By so doing it influenced the lives of the powerful leaders of the time.

The oracle was basically a 'post planted into the ground with the figure of a man at its head, badly carved and badly formed.'[13] Its overall height was not more than that of an average man. It was housed in a rectangular shaped construction that was made from small adobes. The enclosure had six metre tall ramparts that were covered with an adobe plaster. In turn the plaster was decorated with anthropomorphic figures of fish, birds and plants. The figures were painted in red and yellow colours and outlined in black.

After the fall of the Inca Empire the temple was abandoned but despite of this the site continued to have an imposing presence both physically and spiritually on the local population.

During our visit, there was an opportunity to walk up an extensive ramp, which allowed access to the top of the main adobe pyramid. At the time when the Incas occupied the site, anyone climbing to the very top was required to have fasted for a year. Thankfully for us, that requirement was no longer enforced!

The middle aged couple chose to wait in the coach but our guide, the senorita and myself walked the distance to the top. For the most part the two ladies chatted away in Spanish whilst I took in the views. At the summit we were rewarded with a splendid panoramic view that looked out towards Miraflores in the one direction and the Pacific Ocean in another.

Our guide explained that archaeologists believed that human sacrifices had taken place here. She showed us some adobe seats where vestal virgins had sat during the ceremonies. [See Photo No 42] I looked at the adobe seats which faced the far off Pacific Ocean. My mind momentarily transported me back to the time of the Incas and their priests. I was moved to think that the view could possibly be the same that the young girls had witnessed, all those centuries ago. However, there was one big difference. For them, it must have been the last time they saw it.

Returning to ground level, just enough time was allowed for a brief visit to the interesting onsite museum. After which the coach made its return journey to Miraflores.

During the day I had inquired from our guide, about a possible booking for a tour of the old City of Lima. This of course was to make up for the one I had missed on my arrival in Peru. On our return to Miraflores I inquired again if there was any news about my possible booking. The guide casually assured me that a place had already been booked! Furthermore, a coach would meet me in two days time. It would arrive at the same pickup point I had used earlier that day! Such efficiency impressed me no end.

SECOND VISIT TO BARRANCO

It may be said that transport in Lima is both varied and regular. There is the metro-bus that links the various suburbs with the city centre. Then there are the local buses, which I confess I never used and also there are two types of taxi. By far the easiest form of travel in the Lima area, is by taxi. But what I discovered is that there are taxis and there are taxis!

The one type looks every bit like a traditional taxi with its modern livery and uniform paint colour. It also has both visible and legible signs stating that it actually is a taxi. But it can prove to be expensive and therefore it is a good idea to be aware of the type used by some of the local people. This taxi is less obvious in its appearance due to a sparcity of signage and an equal lack of modernity. But they can offer a large saving in the cost of a fare. In the light of this knowledge they are fairly easy to identify. A further clue to their identity is that when looking for business, they normally proceed more slowly than other cars. But what is more obvious than anything, is their unkempt appearance. Yes, they do look somewhat scruffy on the outside but inside is another matter! These taxis are aimed at the lower income group. They provide a service but without the frills. Having said that I hasten to add they are licensed and registered but I can only hope that they are road worthy. Anyway, the cost of travel is considerably less than their refined cousins and they are readily available.

Ever since yesterday, when I got a fleeting glimpse of Barranco, I was infused with a desire to return and to see more of it. It was June the thirteenth and the use of a 'pauper taxi' to get me there seemed like a good idea. Whilst standing on the main street in Miraflores, I didn't have long to wait before one came along. The fact that I was looking in the direction of the oncoming taxi, albeit from a distance, was enough for the driver to be alerted. As the vehicle drew closer to me, my eyes and those of the driver met. With a quick nod of my head, the taxi responded by pulling into the kerb. I was patently aware that before climbing into any taxi I needed to confirm where I was to be taken. But most importantly, to negotiate the cost of the fare. Once the price was agreed I climbed into the back seat.

As I mentioned earlier, the inside of the taxi was 'another matter.' The seat was loose and covered in dust. The upholstery was torn and there were various sorts of rubbish strewn about. Included in the list were a few tin cans and even some straw! I thought to myself all I need now is a sheep to keep me company! The driver, on the other hand, was courteous. Surprisingly, he drove quite well, considering the intermittent loud thuds emanating from underneath the car. I guessed they were due to the lack of adequate suspension.

Within a few minutes we arrived in the centre of Barranco and were very close to the City Hall. I saw what looked like an old railway carriage. It was parked in a prominent position and next to a public walkway. It was there I asked the driver to drop me off. I was standing on the Avenue Prolongacion, San Martin and next to a retired and ornate, nineteenth century railway carriage.

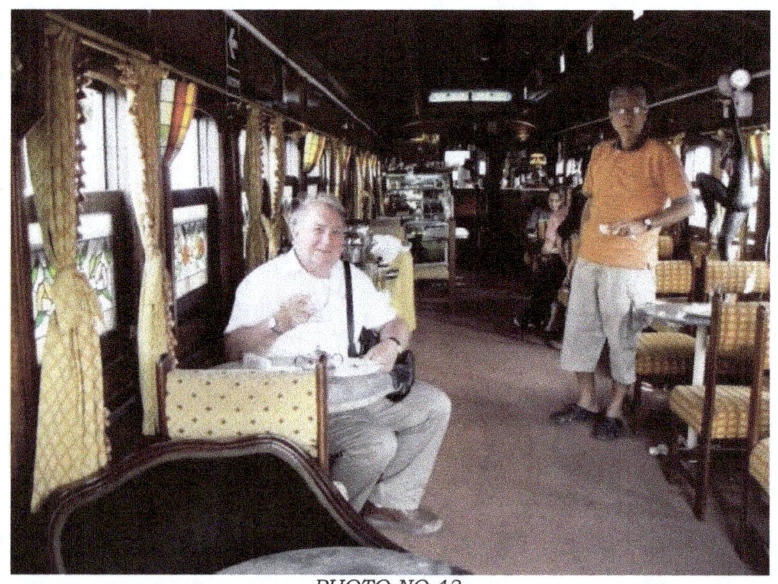

PHOTO NO 43
COFFEE AND CAKE IN A PERUVIAN RAILWAY CARRIAGE

It had been cleverly converted into a unique restaurant with a bar. As I climbed on board I noticed a name printed in bold letters on one side of the carriage. It read, 'Café Cultural Expreso Virgen De Guadalupe.' A smiling waiter offered me a menu that reflected a choice of typical international and Peruvian fare. It all looked tempting but what I needed for the moment was a cup of coffee and a piece of cake! Both arrived in due course and I was not to be disappointed.

As always in Peru, the coffee tasted lovely but the cake was in a word, 'divine.' The word 'divine' is something of a cliché but I assure the reader that the sponge cake was as light as a feather. It was dusted with cinnamon and had a layer of fresh cream that simply melted in my mouth. It was the freshest and most delightful cake I have EVER tasted. What contributed further to my enjoyment, was the surrounding ambience of nineteenth century Peruvian décor. Albeit I was sitting inside a railway carriage!

****

From my previous visit to Barranco, I remembered I had seen what looked like an actual tram car. It was standing on the main road. Since my appetite had been satisfied, for the time being at any rate, I decided to search for it. Walking along the Avenue Pedro de Osma it wasn't long before it came into view. Sure enough it was parked on the road. Surprisingly though what I hadn't previously seen was a kilometre of tram track that it was parked upon. It turned out that this was one of the last electrically operated trams in Peru. At certain times of the week it gave powered rides to anyone wanting the experience. Unfortunately for me my timing was wrong and no rides were to be given on that day.

However, so the saying goes, as one door closes another one opens. I spotted what for me was a bonus that stood on the opposite side of the Avenue. It was in the form of a building having the words 'Museo de la Electricidad' emblazoned above its entrance. It was a museum that broadly speaking reflected the history of electricity in Lima. Inside was like an Aladdin's cave having different items of electrical apparatus. These included various old radio and television sets, the like of which I had long forgotten. One of the television sets was named 'Admiral' and was fitted with four stylish wooden legs. Standing next to it was two impressive looking Wurlitzer Juke Boxes. How I remember many years ago seeing and hearing such things; as they stood in a corner of some smoky coffee bar. But for me, it has to be said, the star of the show was a 1956 model called the 'Centennial.' It boasted the words 'True High Fidelity Music' that were placed in plastic letters next to its record rack. As I was looking through a list of record titles, that could be played on the machine, a man appeared from what seemed like nowhere. It transpired that he was the Curator of the museum. For the princely sum of one Sol he offered to play a record of my choice. Considering the 'Beatles' have always been a favourite of mine I chose their recording of 'And I Love Her.' The Curator placed my coin into a money-slot on the front of the cabinet. He proceeded to select the chosen disc. He did this by pressing two buttons. The one having a number printed on it and the other having a letter. The machine sprung into life and a mechanical arm extracted the selected disc from the record rack. It placed it onto the revolving turntable. A metallic arm lifted from its resting place and moved gracefully across the machine's playing area. It slowly descended onto the disc and music began to play. The sound that emanated from the 'Box' was truly amazing and my mind was instantly transported in time to the 1960's.

THE BEAUTY AND THE BRIDGE

A short while later I wandered down the road to find a viewing point, from where I might observe the distant Pacific Ocean. By doing so I had occasion, once again, to cross the famous Puente de los Suspiros.(Bridge of Sighs)

This time it was void of people and my passage across it was totally unhindered. Whilst walking along I began to think of the wish I had made the day before. Suddenly, and to my utter surprise, a strange sight beheld my eyes. Walking, or rather bouncing towards me, was what looked like a dame, from some English theatre's pantomime. It was in fact a Peruvian gentleman dressed as a voluptuous woman! 'She' was wearing a brightly coloured patterned dress. Two enormous 'boobs' bounced on 'her' chest. At 'her' rear was a similar sized pair of buttocks. They bounced in sympathy with 'her' bust. I was completely dumbfounded. A black curly wig completed the deceitful image. But there was no mistaking a pair of trousers worn on the lower part of the body. "Wait a minute" I declared to myself, "I haven't made a wish this time around, so surely this is not of my doing?" The feminine figure approached me speaking in Spanish. Judging by the accompanying gestures it was evident that I was expected to hand over some money.

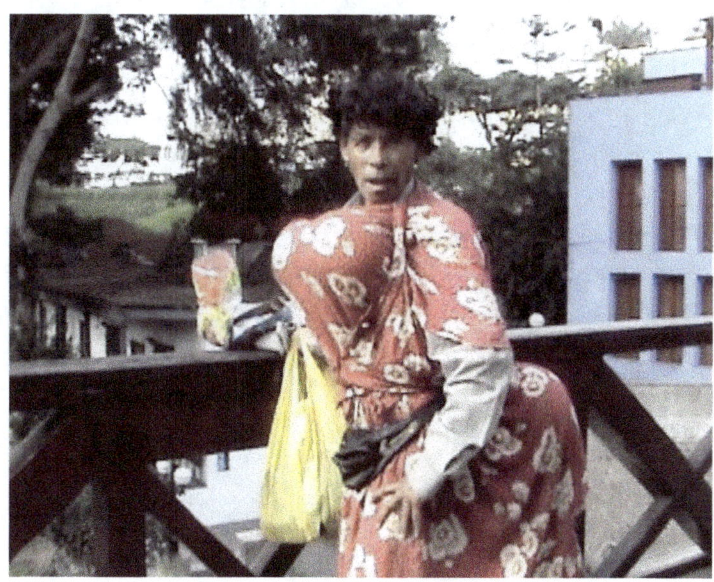

PHOTO NO 44
THE BEAUTY AND THE BRIDGE

131

Remembering the saying, 'discretion is the better part of valour', I decided that rather than dismiss the fellow outright, I would compromise. With that I asked the character to pose for a photo and then I offered some coinage. Flashing me a smile of appreciation the 'beauty on the bridge' took the money and gleefully bounced away into the distance. It appeared that my growing embarrassment had been spared. But then I started to wonder. Was the 'dame' the answer to my wish of yesterday? I like to think not!

TOUR OF OLD LIMA CITY CENTRE

Today was June the fourteenth and I intended to take a guided tour of the old Lima city. As I waited at the end of Independencia Street for my transport to arrive, eight nuns rounded the corner at which I was standing. Like a string of white pearls they passed me in single file. Each was dressed in a white gown and having a matching head dress. Individually they each bade me a 'Buenos dias' (Good day) and I in turn greeted them. I thought how refreshingly polite and pleasant the unexpected encounter had been.

Lima is the capital city of Peru and was founded in 1535 by the Spanish Conquistador, Francisco Pizarro. It lies along the banks of the Rimac River. According to the guide books the average temperature in summer is 24 degrees Celsius; while in winter it is 15 degrees. Overlooking the Pacific Ocean, this 'City of the Kings,' named after the Biblical, 'Three Wise Men', has rapidly transformed into a cosmopolitan melting pot. It is rich with a variety of cultures while maintaining its Peruvian heritage.

The coach arrived safely in Lima, with myself and its passengers, who numbered around fourteen. We began a short walking tour of selected parts of the city.

We were guided to the main square or as they say in Spanish, the 'Plaza Mayor.' It is considered to be the most important location in the capital, since it was the scene of some important historical events.

From here, in the year 1821, the Act of Independence of Peru was proclaimed. It is surrounded by a mix of large and impressive looking buildings, which includes the Presidential Palace. The Palace has housed all Viceroys and Presidents of Peru since it was originally built centuries ago. Some of the buildings are painted in a rather curious mustard colour which is pleasant to view and most certainly eye catching. Others such as the Lima Cathedral have retained their original stone appearance.

The square itself covers an area that would accommodate several tennis courts and is laid out as though it was carpeted with square stone slabs and all fitting neatly together.

Many oblong-shaped gardens are placed symmetrically about the square, looking like continents embossed on a map of the world. Each is surrounded by a single linked-chain that is supported at regular intervals, with vertically placed steel tubes.

A number of the garden areas have planted in their midst, singular tall and slim palm trees. They offer the visual impression that they might be guards standing to attention. These in turn are surrounded by beds of brightly coloured flowers. Here and there are bold and ornate looking, cast iron lampposts. They have three branches sprouting from their tops and look every bit like candelabra on some old grand piano. Noticeably at one side of the square is a seventeenth century, ornamental bronze fountain. Placed high above it is a statue of the 'Angel of Triumph'.

Aside from the physical attributes of the city there is one surprising feature that should be mentioned.

It is the apparent lack of litter. To accomplish this goal there is an army of uniformed road cleaners that seemingly do their job admirably.

From the square our party made its way towards the next major attraction. It was the San Francisco Convent. En route to this place of worship we made a slight deviation. We stopped at the corner of Calle De Pescaderia and entered into a restaurant called 'El Cordano.' For over a hundred years this quaint little eating place has been tending to the culinary needs of the local citizens. In more recent times it caters for the ever growing number of visitors from far afield.

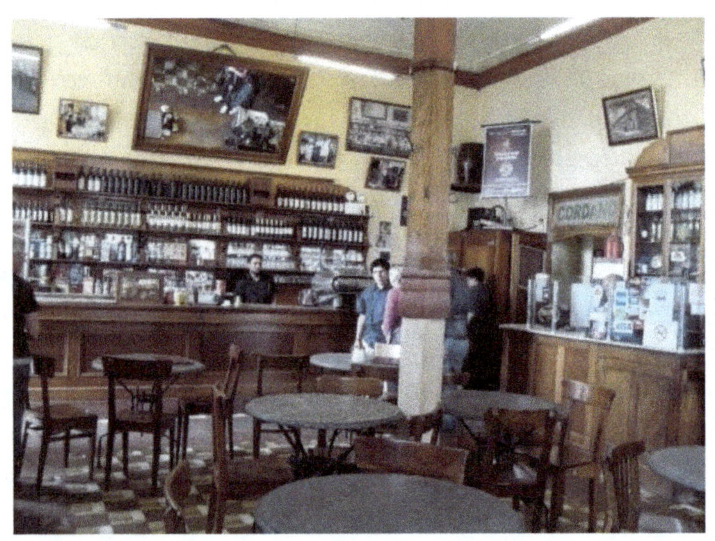

PHOTO NO 45
INSIDE THE EL CORDANO RESTAURANT

I'm told that the food is tasty and traditional, serving amongst other things, lovely cream cakes, coffee and a range of alcoholic drinks. An enduring national favourite to try, so I am informed, is the traditional 'lomo saltado.' There is also the 'Jamon del Norte' which is a thickly cut, ham sandwich served with onions.

To wash it down one can order a glass of chilled Chicha. The latter is a purple coloured corn beer, having low alcohol content. However, ours was just a fleeting visit born out of interest and not intended to refresh ourselves. Even so it was worth the visit to soak up the ambience that reflected the old world charm of Peru.

Having moved on from the restaurant I chanced to see more of the Lima Police Force. This time they appeared as a line of riot police standing next to a building. They stood with their long shields poised upright and their protective helmets hanging from their belts. I supposed they stood in readiness for any action. But safe to say, there was no threat from our party!

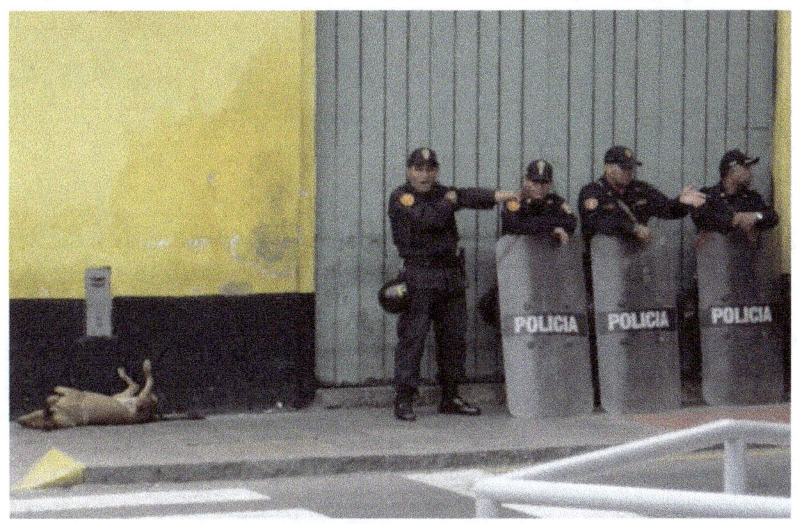

PHOTO NO 46
RIOT POLICE WITH THEIR DOG

What I couldn't help noticing was a dog that lay nearby. It was on its back and had its legs pointing into the air. It gave me the impression that it was out for the count. I quietly wondered if it might be a victim of police brutality or perhaps more correctly, it was just a police dog stealing (sic) forty winks!

At the end of a short but brisk walk from the El Cordano restaurant, we arrived at the Convent of San Francisco. The magnificent edifice was constructed just a few years after the foundation of Lima. In front of its entrance door is a court yard that hosts a little fountain which adds beauty to the façade. Pigeons are in abundance here and visitors often spend a few minutes in tossing some food in their direction. Vendors are about, with packets of seed for sale, to supply the compassionate tourists. The architectonic complex is made up by the church and the convent of San Francisco, as well as of the chapels of the Solitude and the Miracle.

As our party walked along the cloisters, I marvelled at the elaborate murals that decorated the walls. I also saw some patios adorned with Sevillian tiles. Photography was strictly forbidden inside the buildings and staff members watched like hawks for any offenders. We were taken to the library that looked like a scene from a Harry Potter movie. Its dark polished wooden shelving was many decades in age. It supported hundreds of valuable books and manuscripts of undoubted importance. Many of the books are made from sheets of velum or young goat skin. They have lettering that is coated in gold leaf that reflects the light. Because of this they are known as the 'enlightened' or 'illuminate'. It was hardly surprising to learn that this building is the headquarters of Lima's Museum of Religious Art.

Our visit was brought to a climax by taking us beneath the church buildings where there is a network of underground galleries and catacombs. Originally there was a cemetery on the site but today hundreds of bones of the deceased are on view for all to see. Concrete walkways made the movement from one area to another fairly effortless but there were a few arches that required us to stoop a little.

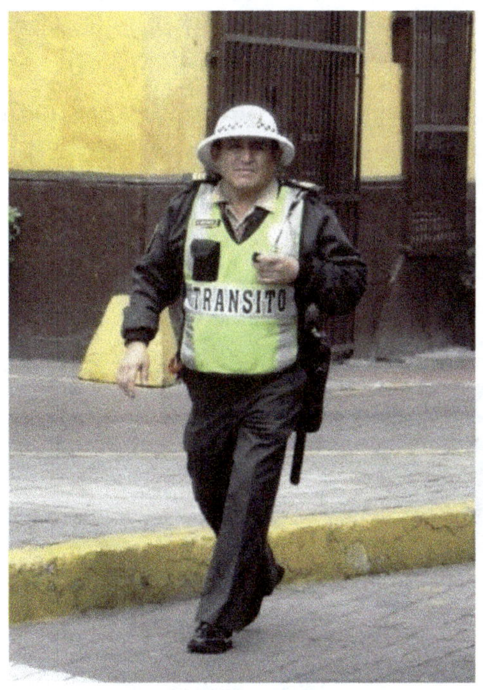

PHOTO NO 47
A FRIENDLY TRAFFIC COP

The skulls were pointing inward and all were linked by the femur and tibia bones from human limbs. I thought that if only the skulls could speak what a fascinating tale they could tell.

Before much time had passed we were outside the building and standing in the bright daylight. It felt good to breathe the fresh air. Our group purchased a few souvenir postcards at a small but well stocked shop. Afterwards we boarded a coach that was to ferry us to our next and final port of call. It was to be the Museum of Lima. Fortunately, our departure was eased along by the help from a local traffic cop, who sported yet another style of police uniform.

The Museum of Lima is not far from the Cathedral complex and is filled with many interesting artefacts. Collectively they attempt to tell the history of Peru. But in the limited time that our group was allowed, it was impossible to see them all. Although the ones that we saw were strangely fascinating. Of particular delight to me was a water vessel known as a whistling pitcher.

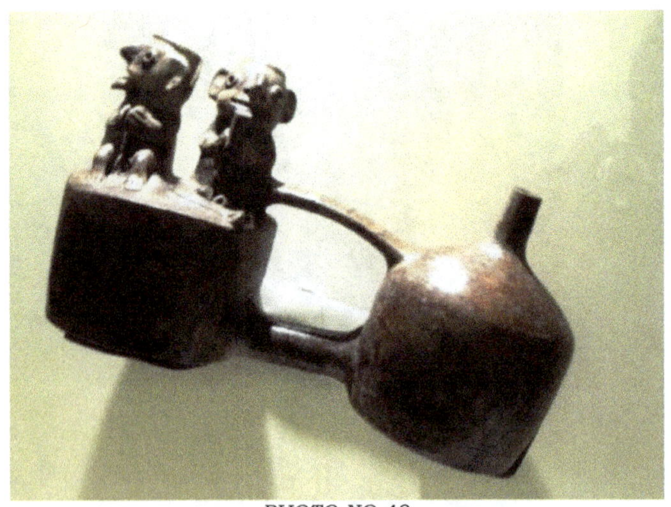

PHOTO NO 48
A WHISTLING PITCHER

THE WHISTLING PITCHER

The photo No 48 shows an example of the unusual vessel. Two large water containers are shown in the photograph. One on the left and the other on the right. They are joined together by two lengths of ceramic material. The upper most length is fashioned as a carrying handle and is of a solid construction. Whereas the lower one is tubular in design, which allows for the free flow of water from one container to the other. The container on the right has a spout on its top which allows it to be partially filled with water.

In this example, when the pitcher is tilted forward, water flows from the right hand container and through the connecting tube. It enters the container on the left which is void of water but contains normal air. As the water enters the container it pushes the air upwards which is then compressed.

At the top of the left hand container are two cleverly designed outlet ducts. In this example they are disguised by the moulded figures. The compressed air is forced through small holes that are present in the ducts. The air acts in much the same way as a flute that is being played. Depending on the interior design, the sounds produced generally imitate those of birds. Archaeologists know from images of musicians depicted on many textiles and ceramics, that music was important to the ancient people of South America.

At ceremonial areas of Cahuachi, archaeological finds have included instruments such as flutes and drums. Based on these finds it is believed that music was used during religious rituals and ceremonies. There have been a number of occasions when examples of whistling pitchers have been found at grave sites. This has given rise to the notion that the items may have been used to make a melodious sound during the funeral ceremony.

STRING QUIPUS

Another item displayed within the museum and one which I found fascinating, was an example of a 'Quipu.' The ancient population of South America were known not to have any form of writing. But they did have a means by which they could transfer a large quantity of information and across great distances of land. The Incas have left us with examples of what they call 'quipus.' They are essentially pieces of coloured strings of varying lengths, that are tied together at one end in a way that resembles a bunch of keys. The individual lengths of string have knots tied in them at a number of different points. It is believed that the Incas recorded numeric data and other information on quipus. By varying the position or colour of the knots and strings, complex messages were recorded. They could only be read by trained 'quipucamayocs', which is a name given to the person who could decipher the information. Specially selected runners would carry the quipu from one place to another and sometimes cover many miles. In this way information was shared. The surviving quipus are dated at between 1200AD and 1532AD.

****

The visit to the museum marked the end of the day's tour and the coach set off in the direction of Miraflores. Along the way people were delivered to their respective hotels. It was during this process I discovered that the Pacific Ocean was not far from where I lived. That evening I made my way along the road and down to the beach. 'Down' was the operative word. I had to descend hundreds of steps down a cliff face to reach the literal sea level. The sight of the sea was breath taking. Long crested waves slowly rolled towards me as I stood on the pebbled beach. Surfers, who amounted to about a dozen, practised their skills as I watched. There was a small pier that poked out from the beach and towards the horizon. Perched on it and reflecting the rays of the setting sun, were what looked like a cluster of shops. I couldn't resist the desire to walk along it. Almost at the end of the pier was 'La Rosa Nautica,' a restaurant that was noted for selling fresh fish dishes. Throughout my holiday, whenever the mention of a fish meal cropped up, this particular restaurant was highly recommended. The timing was right and I thought "Why Not?"

I chose from the menu what I considered to be the best value for money. 'Ceviche' was pieces of raw fish, with pieces of octopus and scallops, all cured in citrus juice and seasoned with peppers. Along with the restaurant this was a meal that was also highly recommended.

Minutes after placing the order a waiter arrived with a bowl of heated bread rolls together with a glass of agua. (water) The main dish eventually arrived. It comprised of the fish pieces that were mixed with lettuce, sliced onions and some nuts thrown in for good measure. The food in itself was fine but I found the lemon juice, in which it was served, to be a problem.

Had the fish been alive, it would have had a wonderful swimming pool in which to exercise! The food was swamped with the lemon juice. My taste buds tingled like they had been anesthetised by a dentist's needle. I could hardly taste the fish for the flavour of lemon. It was then I realised why the agua had been provided!

When it came time to pay the bill, I had already made a mental calculation of the cost. The charge was much more than I thought. "What is this extra amount for?" I queried.

"Oh; that is for the bread rolls and water" answered the manager. I was not amused!

The walk, or should I say climb, back to my hotel was harder than the outward journey. It had been relatively easy to descend the hundreds of steps from the town to the beach. However, retracing the route was an ordeal. It took several minutes of breathless climbing, to gain the top of the stone-stepped stairway.

About this time the sun had set and darkness had descended. Lights on the street lamps were shining and people were milling about. They appeared to be either on their way home from work or were going shopping.

I walked along an empty pavement. In the distance I caught sight of an adult couple, with a boy of about fourteen years of age. They were walking towards me. Suddenly the boy broke away from the couple and approached me at some speed. He was wearing a pair of roller blades. A popular form of mechanised footwear. He looked as though he was going to knock me over. But with only a few inches between us he stopped abruptly. Perhaps guessing I was an English tourist he spoke in English. With a beaming smile on his face he said, "Hello my name is Sancha Cruz." Balancing himself on his blades he began shuffling a deck of cards. "I do magic" he announced, "Would you like to see a card trick?"

Having got over my initial shock I glanced over his shoulder. The couple were looking on approvingly. "Sure", I said, "Why not?" He then asked me to choose a card, as he held out the splayed pack in his hands. From one end of the pack I chose the eight of hearts. He took the card from me. Without me losing sight of his hands, he placed the card into the middle of the pack. Then he closed them altogether. The full pack of cards were held in one hand and with all the cards facing downwards. He asked me to declare the value of my chosen card. When I announced its identity he proceeded to turn the top card over. Sure enough there was my eight of hearts!

"Very clever", I thought. Perhaps someday 'Sancha Cruz' might be seen performing on Peruvian television.

HUACA PUCLLANA

It was June the fifteen and there was two days remaining before my return to England.

One of the many brochures I had acquired mentioned a historical site called 'Huaca Pucllana'. Following a little research, I was amazed to learn that it was actually within walking distance from my hotel. Pucllana is a name given to a great ceremonial centre built by people from the Lima culture between 200AD and 700AD. The word 'Huaca' refers to a burial mound or religious site.

At the ceremonial centre small adobe bricks were made by hand and placed in vertical rows to create walls and platforms. The walls were constructed with ten metre wide trapezoidal panels. They formed plazas, having ramps and enclosures. Aside from these, a great adobe brick wall was built running from North to South. It separated the two important areas within the complex. To the east of the wall was the administrative sector that had many plazas and enclosures that were possibly used for public meetings. To the west of the wall was the ceremonial sector. In this area can be found a pyramid and plazas where religious ceremonies took place.

Much of the centre has been restored and excavations continue to uncover artefacts which include mummies. I spent an hour or two looking around the various structures and marvelling at their enormity. There was an on-site museum that I found to be absorbing. Inside it were displayed numerous examples of pottery that had been excavated at the site. They were decorated in a style that was unique to the Lima people of that time. Their religious world was greatly influenced by the sea and is reflected in the patterns painted on their pottery.

A two-headed shark painted on an earthenware jar is just one famous example.

A PAINFUL DAY

On the morning of June the sixteenth, as I climbed out of bed, a sudden pain shot across the small of my back. It was something akin to an electric shock. The pain that followed was acute and it persisted. Some years ago I injured my lower back in a fall from a ladder. As a result both periodically and unpredictably, my lower back muscles might go into a spasm. The outcome is considerable pain. Since the original accident I always pack a tube of pain relieving gel into my holiday suitcase. With considerable effort I managed to apply some gel to the afflicted area. By mid afternoon I was sufficiently recovered to leave the hotel and shuffle to the end of the street. There I found a small park area and lowered my aching body onto a park bench. It was then that the gentle warmth of the sunshine brought some relief. On my return journey I enjoyed a hot meal at a local café and finally, when I got back to my hotel room, I rested until the following day.

THE COUNTDOWN FOR HOME

Sunlight slowly lit up my bedroom at the dawn of yet another Peruvian day. June the seventeenth had begun both warm and peaceful but my heart was feeling a tinge of sadness. It was to be the last day of my Peruvian adventure. The pain in my back had eased as a result of the previous hours of rest. But although able to walk fairly well, I considered my lower back to be like a dormant volcano. It was treated with the upmost respect. After packing most of my meagre possessions I wandered down to the breakfast area for the last time. My choice of table was one facing the open sky.

I contemplated what I needed to do before leaving for the airport. Seconds later my mind re-focused on the immediate surroundings. Sitting at a table in front of me, was a tall and well dressed Afro-American gent. Speaking in Spanish and perhaps almost instinctively by this time, I called out the words "Buenos dias." (Good day) I did so in a louder than normal voice. I wanted to make sure that the man heard me. A hand that was about to place food into his mouth, moved lethargically down towards the table. He turned his head slightly in my direction and casually uttered the word, "Hi."

Before long we were engaged in conversation and I learned that his name was 'Brad.' He had travelled from the United States of America to Peru, to conduct a business deal. I gathered he wasn't too happy with the USA Government. This became more evident when I broached the subject of racism. I asked him if such was still active in his country. He replied as though the answer went without saying. Almost with a sigh he said, "Hell; yeah!"

During our talk a breakfast was diligently delivered to my table. The chef played different roles to keep the hotel running smoothly. Cooking, as well as serving my daily omelette, was just two of them. Brad finished his food and then politely excused himself. As he was leaving he announced in his distinctive American drawl, "It was nice talkin' to ya."

After breakfast I did some last minute shopping. Along the way I decided to visit what was by now, my favourite destination. It was of course, Kennedy Park. It is said that history repeats itself and whilst visiting the park I believe it most certainly did. It happened that a shoeshine man approached me with determination and offered to clean my shoes. I thought where had that happened before?

As I was about to say no, I suddenly remembered the guilt I had experienced after refusing the man at Lima central. This time I readily agreed. The man set to work diligently with his brush and cloths. He applied in turn some liquid polish from his collection of bottles. Slowly my travel weary shoes were transformed. They were made ready for their long journey home. As the man exercised his skills my mind reminisced over the many varied places, and faces, I had recently seen.

There was the Pyramids of Peru; which I never knew existed before this adventure began. I had stood on and flown over the actual Nazca Lines. Sometime later, whilst walking around the Chauchilla Necropolis, a mummified person(s) had apparently 'spoken' to me. A motor boat had taken me on the Pacific Ocean to see the wild birdlife of the Ballestas Islands. At the ancient city of Cusco, I had witnessed the colourful festival of Corpus Christi. At Sacsayhuaman I had walked amongst the enormous stones of the ruined fortress. This spectacle was only surpassed by my time spent at Machu Picchu; the Sacred City of the Incas. Finally, after taking a short taxi ride from my hotel, I had walked in the streets of Barranco. After making a wish, I had crossed its famous 'Bridge of Sighs' and was shocked by the unexpected result! In summing up, during the whole of my adventure, I had flown in seven different aeroplanes; had taken two train journeys and had ridden in various buses and taxis.

Slowly my thoughts were replaced with a realisation. In just a few hours, I would be travelling on yet another journey. This time, it would be one to take me to my modest home in England.

REFERENCES

[1]http:/www.quotations.comquote24004html. [Accessed 30 June 2012]

[2]*Richard Hammond meets Evil Knievel.* First broadcast on BBC 2 TV 23 December 2007

[3]http:/www.go2Peru.comecs3_inghtm. [Accessed 12 July 2012]

[4]http:/www.booking.comhotelpecasa-andina-classic-Nazcahtml?aid=3238i [Accessed 18 July 2012]

[5]*Nazca Paracas Mystery and Nature.* Roberto Gheller Doig. 2010. Lima Peru. pp.28-29.

[6]http:/www.ladatco.comPER%20Cahuachi.htm.[Accessed 21 July 2012]

[7]*Nazca Paracas Mystery and Nature.* Roberto Gheller Doig. 2010. Lima Peru. pp.34-35.

[8]http:/www.bbc.co.uk news uk-11460644 BBC 2012. [Accessed 22 July 2012]

[9]http:/www.enwikipedia.org.wiki.Maria_Reiche [Accessed 22 July 2012]

[10]http:/www.peruboarding.com/Sandboarding/Cerro_Bianco/cerro_binco.html PesnowInc.St.Louis MO 1997-2001. [Accessed 22 July 2012]

[11]*Nazca Paracas Mystery and Nature.* Roberto Gheller Doig.2010.p.9.

[12]*Nazca Paracas Mystery and Nature.* Roberto Gheller Doig.2010.p.9.

[13]*The Conquest of the Incas,* Hemming, John, p.62 (Book Club Associates, London, 1974.)

BIBLIOGRAPHY

Arguedas, J.M.H. & Dukszto, A.,
Machu Picchu The Sacred City, (hipocampo.com 2011)

Doig, R.G., *Nazca Paracas Mystery and Nature,* (Lima, Peru, 2010)

Doig, R.G., *Ancestors of the Incas,* (Lima, Peru, 2005)

Hemming, John, *The Conquest of the Incas,* (Book Club Associates, London, 1974)

A LIST OF HOTELS VISITED BY THE AUTHOR

1. Hotel El Tambo 1 – Miraflores
   [Av La Paz 1276-Miraflores-Lima-Peru]

2. Casa Handina Classic-Nazca-Peru
   [www.casa-andina.com]

3. La Hacienda Bahia – Paracas
   [www.hoteleslahacienda.com/hotel-bahia-paracas]

4. Imperial Palace Mabey Hotel – Cusco
   [www.hotelesmabey.com/en/cusco]

5. Wasi Independencia - Miraflores
   [www.bedandbreakfastmiraflores.com]